The Ultimate Vegan Recipe Book – German-Style

Over 250 Recipes from easy to difficult for Beginners and Professionals

Jonathan M. Hiemer

1st edition

2019

© All rights reserved

Foreword	**15**
Abbreviations	**17**
Starters & Salads	**19**
Pasta Salad	21
Stuffed Avocado	22
Turnip Topinambur Carpaccio	23
Mixed Salad with warm Mushrooms and Honey-Mustard Vinaigrette	25
Baba Ganoush	27
Lentil-Tomato-Salad	28
Antipasti	29
Hot Carrot Salad with Herbs	31
Tomatoes - Olive Relish	33
Hot Melon Skewers	34
Sushi with Tofu	35
Roasted Peppers	36
Beetroot fried with Walnuts and Salad	37
Marinated Asparagus - Strawberry - Salad	38
Avocado - Tatar	39
Zucchini - Tomatoes - Vegetables	40
Falafel	41
Pumpkin Salad	43
Carrots - Apple - Salad with Orange Dressing and Walnuts	44
Carrot Salad with Peanuts	45
Bruschetta	46
Rocket-Carrot and Mango Salad	47
Taboulé	48
Piquant pickled dried Tomatoes	49

Pea Salad with Avocado and Mint	*50*
Avocado - Salsa with jacket Potatoes	*51*
Baked Tofu	*52*
Mediterranean Courgettes	*53*
Italian cucumber Salad	*54*
Fried Garlic - Fennel	*55*
Potato Salad with Apples and Lentils	*56*
Mercimek Köftesi	*57*
Buckwheat - Carrots - Bratlings	*59*
Fruity Bean Salad with Thyme	*60*
Potato Salad	*61*
Avocado Relish	*62*
Lebanese Spinach - Particles	*64*
Radish salad	*66*
Aromatic Spinach Balls	*67*
Zucchini Meatballs	*68*
Pear and Cheese Salad	*69*
Stuffed Pancakes with Spinach, Lentils and Quinoa	*70*
Sweet Potato Tortilla	*71*
Summer Rolls with Peanut Dip	*73*
Summer Salad with fresh Asparagus	*75*
Cheese	*76*
Waldorf Salad	*77*
Vegan meat Salad	*78*

Soups and Stews — **79**

Cream of Pumpkin Soup	*81*
Pumpkin Soup with Ginger and Coconut	*82*
Lentil Potato Stew	*83*
Tomato Soup	*84*

Watermelons - Gazpacho	85
Coconut Soup with Sweet Potatoes	86
Mango Carrot Soup	87
Red lentil Coconut Soup	88
Fine Ginger and Carrot Soup	89
Silesian Potato Soup	90
Almond - Broccoli - Soup	91
Sweet Potato-Banana Soup	92
Broccoli Cream Soup	93
Mushroom Cream Soup	94
Leek Soup	95
Orange-Carrot Soup	96
15 Minutes - Vegetables - Noodles - Soup	97
African Peanut Stew	98
Creamy Beetroot - Carrots - Soup	99
Curry - Ginger - Apple - Soup	100
Potato Soup with Mushrooms	101
Bananas - Coconut - Chili - Soup	102
Lentil Soup	103
Lemon Grass - Coconut Milk - Soup	104
Zucchini - Coconut - Soup	105
Semolina Soup with Vegetables	106
Tofu - Soup	107
Gazpacho	108
Tom Kha Hed Soup	109
Baden-Style Stew	110
Pea Soup	112
Green Garden Soup	113
Vegetable Soup	114

Hearty Minestrone	*115*
Main Courses and Side Dishes	**117**
Vegan Tomato Quiche	*119*
Creamy Peanut Pan with Vegetables and Soya	*121*
Vegan Bratwurst	*123*
Lasagna	*124*
Millet - Scrambled Eggs	*126*
Millet - Pan	*127*
Lemon-Fennel Risotto	*128*
Sunflowercream	*129*
Chili sin Carne	*130*
Chicken Fricassee	*132*
Lentil Bratlings	*133*
Paprika Mortadella	*134*
Pizza with Yeast Melt	*135*
Cream Cheese	*137*
Meatballs with Vegetables	*138*
Meatballs	*139*
Russian minced Meat Pot	*140*
Tortellini with smoked Tofu Spinach filling	*141*
Bulgur Curry	*143*
Spinach Noodle Dough	*144*
Chinese Cabbage Chopping Pan	*145*
Country liver Sausage	*146*
Spaghettini with Cherry Tomatoes and Balsamic Vinegar	*147*
Raw Vegetable Lasagna	*148*
Spaghetti with Sugar Peas and Cherry Tomatoes	*150*
Stuffed Peppers with green Spelt	*151*

Apple red Cabbage	153
Eggplant Ragout	154
Eggplant Spaghetti	155
Cauliflower on Noodles	156
Curry Noodle Pan	157
Steam Noodles	158
Potato Goulash	159
Potato Dumplings	160
Chickpeas and Beans Stew	161
Pumpkin Ragout	162
Schnetzel pan	163
Vegetable Paella	164
Spaghetti with Garlic, Oil and Pepper	165
Hokkaido Pumpkin Lasagna	166
Chili Spinach Risotto with Lemon Grass	168
Pasta Bavette with fresh Mint and Peasauce	169
Mushroom Burger	170
Tofu Schnitzel	172
Bratwurst	173
Beanburger	174
Another Burger, just different.	175
Seitanschnitzel Gypsy style	176
Cauliflower Schnitzel	177
Meatballs	178
Tofu - Meatballs	179
French Fries from the Oven	180
Curry - Vegetables with Tofu	181
Indian Lentil Stew	182
Hack - Noodle - Casserole	183

Pasta Dough	185
Spaghetti Napoli	186
Onion Tart	187
Pizza Garlic Champignon Paprika	188
Dips and Sauces	**189**
Mayonnaise	191
Hummus	192
Paprika Humus	193
Mushroom Dip	194
Creamy-aromatic Ginger-Sesame Dip	195
Greek Fava from Chickpeas	196
Fava from red Lentils	197
Oriental white Bean Paste	198
Tomato-Oregano-Pesto	199
Guacamole	200
Avocado - Mustard - Dip	201
Auberginepuree	202
South African Mango - Chili - Relish	203
Aubergine onion spread	204
Wild garlic Pesto	205
Béchamel sauce for Lasagne	206
Currysauce	207
Peanutsauce	208
Spring Soybean curd Cheese	209
Low Fat Potato Mayo	210
Ketchup	211
Brownsauce	212
Nut Bolognese	213
Dried Tomatoes - Nut - Pesto	214

Mushroom - Pesto	215
Walnutpaste	216
Tapenade	217
Quince - Horseradish - Chutney	218
Aubergine cream with Sesamepaste	219
Salsa	220
Gypsysauce	221
Aioli	222
Apple - Figs - Chutney	223
Sesamesauce	224
Desserts	**225**
Chocolate Mousse	227
Sweet Pancakes	228
Tiramisu	229
Strawberry Ice Cream	231
Strawberry Shake	232
Peanut Cream	233
Semolina Porridge	234
Hazelnut Ice Cream	235
Chocolate Ice Cream	236
Fruit Ice Cream with Tofu	237
Bananas - Coconut - Ice Cream	238
Banana Ice Cream	239
Coconut Pudding	240
Crepes	241
Oranges - Spice Pancakes	242
Banana Pancakes	243
Wild berries - Smoothie	244
Chocolates - Peanutbutter - Tofu - Pudding	245

Tofu Fruit Cream	246
Cashew Cream	247
Wholemeal spelt Waffles	248
Microwave Cup Cake	249
Winter Orange Sorbet	250
Vanilla pudding	252
Halva	253
Tofu Ragout with Pears and Rosemary	255
Lemon Yoghurt	256
Strawberrysorbet	257
Sweet Spring Rolls	258
Avocado - Sorbet	259
Apricots - Marsala - Sorbet	260
Chocolate Banana Tofu Cream	261
Chocolate-Avocado Mousse	262
Coconut Apricot Balls	263

Grilling   **264**

Grilled Vegetables	266
Grilled Vegetables - Salad	267
Oven Potato BBQ Style	268
Fiery grilled Potato Skewers	269
Grilled Fennel	270
Grilled Pita Bread	271
Tofu - Skewers	272
Grilled Asparagus	273
Grill Marinade	274
Grilled Mangoes with Raspberry Sauce	275
Tsatsiki	276
Mediterranean hot Sauce	277

Grilled Pumpkin	*278*
Tofu Fruit Skewers	*278*
Grilled Steak	*278*
Steak again different	*279*
Focaccia	*281*
Potato Salad with Spring Onions	*282*
Grilled Mushrooms	*283*
Garlic Puree with Thyme	*284*
Cucumbers - Salsa	*285*
Zucchini - Tomatoes - Onion - Skewers	*286*
Grilled Avocado	*287*
Grilled Courgette with Mint	*288*
Baking	**289**
Chocolate - Nut - Coconut - Cake	*291*
Russian Plucked Cake	*292*
Vegan Walnut Cake	*293*
Chocolate Mocha Cake	*294*
Red Wine Cake	*295*
Orange Ccake	*296*
Chocolate Cake (gluten free)	*297*
Chocolate Cheesecake without baking	*299*
Apple Pie with Cinnamon Sprinkles	*300*
Marzipan Cake	*301*
Cinnamon Stars	*303*
Biscuit - Basic Recipe	*304*
Chocolate Muffins	*305*
Blueberry Muffins	*306*
Cheesecake Muffins	*307*
Apple Muffins	*308*

Raisin Mares	309
Pita - Bread with Sesame Seeds	310
Pizza Bread	311
Baguette Parisienne	312
Gingerbread	313
Fruit Bbread	314
Covered Apple Pie	315
Oat Biscuits	316
Raspberry Pudding Cake	317
Potato Bbread	318
Carrot Cake	319
Cherry Crumble	320
Coconut Cookies	322
Pumpkin Seed Bread	323
Covered Plum Cake	324
Onion Tart	325
Oat Flake Nut Biscuits	327
Tortillas	328
Banana Bread	329
Coarse Rye Bread	330
Wholemeal Bread	332
Buns	333
Pumpkin - Olives - Rosemary - Bread	334
Wholemeal roll with Carrots and Sunflower Seeds	335
Cereal Rolls	337
Tomato and Olive Ciabatta	339

Disclaimer   **341**

Copyright   **342**

Imprint **343**

Foreword

First of all, I would like to thank you for choosing my cookbook "The "ultimate" vegan recipe book". I'm sure it will give you a lot of pleasure.

But I must entrust you with something - I am not a great writer who makes many words. Therefore, I will keep it very factual in this cookbook and present you the reason why you bought my vegan cookbook: Because of the recipes!

It is also far away from me to tell you something about the philosophy of the vegans. You won't read anything about how great and healthy it is to practice vegan life. You have probably already informed yourself about this extensively elsewhere and therefore do not need any more information reading from me or are living vegan yourself for a long time and are only looking for new recipes.

What I will give you with this cookbook are delicious vegan dishes.

Whether you're an "old" vegan professional or just recently immersed in vegan life, you'll find that being vegan is an adventure you have to get involved with every day. Finding recipes isn't always easy, and once you've found what you're looking for, they should taste good as well.

I am sure that you will find something in this cookbook and that many of the recipes will grow into your gourmet heart. You will also learn that it is not always necessary to use tofu or soy for all dishes.

Go on a delicious culinary journey, which this cookbook will reveal to you. From starters to soups and main courses, baking and grilling, to delicious desserts. There is something for everyone here.

However, I have to disappoint you if you are looking for photos of finished dishes in this cookbook. There are none!

And deliberately not. Because I do not only want to stimulate your desire to eat, but also your fantasy.

I would like you to bring your fantasy into play. Don't just cook a dish from a cookbook, cook YOUR dish.

It doesn't matter if the delicious casserole has 4 or 6 layers or if the mayonnaise is more yellowish or snow-white. Everyone knows what a stew or tiramisu has to look like.

Cook and enjoy with all your senses and in my opinion fantasy also counts.

Just start right away - surprise yourself and your loved ones and let your imagination run wild.

Abbreviations

On this page you will find all the abbreviations you will find in the cookbook. If I should have forgotten one or the other unit, then I ask for excuse!

Just send me an eMail to hiemerjonathan@gmail.com and I will add it in the next update.pck = pack st. = piece

g = gram

kg = kilogram

ml = millilitre

cm = centimetre

cl = centiliter

l = litre

kcal = kilocalories

possibly = possibly

approx. = Circa

m. gr. = medium large

1sp. = knife **Tip**

tl = teaspoon

el = tablespoon

T = cup

gestr. = painted

go. = clustered

n.B. = as required

Starters & Salads

Pasta Salad

Ingredients

500 g vegan noodles (Fusilli), 2 pck soy cream, 1 pck smoked tofu, 1 can peas, 100 g black olives, 1 can corn, 1 bunch spring onions, ½ lemon, the juice thereof (optional), vegetable oil, salt water, some red wine vinegar, salt and pepper, some Maggi, some cayenne pepper

Preparation

Cook the noodles in salted water until al dente and then rinse with cold water.

Cut the tofu into small cubes and fry them in neutral oil until they are slightly brown. Remove the smoked tofu from the pan. Leave the oil in the pan. Do not save the oil so that the pasta salad does not get too dry.

Now add the soy cream to the oil in the pan and bring to the boil. Then season the sauce with vinegar, salt, pepper and 2 - 3 spritzers of Maggi and if desired with lemon. Add cayenne pepper and olives.

Drain corn and peas, rinse and drain. Now cut the spring onions into rings and add everything (incl. noodles) with the sauce.

Stir. Ready!

Stuffed Avocado

Ingredients

1 ripe avocado, 1 tomato, 1 tablespoon onion, 4 tablespoons olive oil, 2 tablespoons balsamic vinegar, 4-6 leaf-fresh basil, 1 teaspoon dried oregano, salt and pepper, green salad

Preparation

Cut the avocado in half lengthwise and remove the core.

Season the avocado halves with salt and pepper.

Cut the tomato and onions into small cubes and add to the halves. Fill with olive oil and balsamic vinegar and sprinkle with the herbs.

Arrange on salad leaves and serve with a spoon.

Turnip Topinambur Carpaccio

Ingredients

4 Jerusalem artichokes, 1 turnip, 1 orange juice, ½ the juice of half a lemon, 1 dash of orange blossom water, 20 hazelnuts, roughly chopped, some olive oil, some salt, pepper, black, from the mill, some leaves of mint

Preparation

Peel the root vegetables and cut them into very thin slices, then arrange them on a plate.

Using a blender, make a creamy vinaigrette from the juice and olive oil.

Flavor with orange blossom water, salt & pepper. Drizzle the vegetables with the vinaigrette and garnish with the mint leaves and the hazelnuts.

Fun Fact

Jerusalem artichoke (Helianthus tuberosus) is a plant of the family of composite flowers (Asteraceae) and belongs to the same genus as sunflower (Helianthus annuus).

It is a useful plant whose root tuber is primarily used for nutrition. The taste of the Jerusalem artichoke tubers is sweet, the consistency is watery, and it is reminiscent of artichoke bottoms.

The tuber can be eaten raw in salads or cooked in saltwater. They are also suitable for eating fried like potatoes. A juice can also be prepared as a drink. It can be thickened in an acidic environment and produces a 90% fructose syrup. The golden yellow to brown Jerusalem artichoke syrup is sold as an alternative sweetener. Particularly noteworthy is the ingredient inulin, an indigestible polysaccharide. As a water-soluble dietary fibre, inulin is an important prebiotic. The inulin content is highest at the time of harvest and decreases during storage. The total sugar content (in terms of mass) remains constant.

Mixed Salad with warm Mushrooms and Honey-Mustard Vinaigrette

Ingredients

½ Head iceberg lettuce, 2 peppers, red and yellow, 1 tin of corn, well drained, 250 g cocktail tomatoes, red and yellow, 500 g brown mushrooms, 1 red onion, 1 teaspoon vegetable stock, 250 ml water, 5 tablespoons balsamic vinegar, 1 tablespoon olive oil, 2 tablespoons mustard of your choice, 2 tablespoons agave syrup, 1 handful of seasonal herbs, salt and coloured pepper, oil for frying

Preparation

Wash the iceberg lettuce, drain and cut into small pieces.

Wash the peppers, remove the seeds and cut into small strips.

Wash and halve or quarter the tomatoes, clean and slice the mushrooms. Finely dice the onion.

Wash the herbs and carefully pat dry, then chop finely and put aside. Bring 250 ml water to the boil and sprinkle in 1 teaspoon vegetable stock.

Heat the oil in a frying pan and sauté the mushrooms briefly, then add the onions and fry briefly. Season to taste with salt and pepper. Deglaze with the vegetable stock and simmer on a low flame until the vegetable stock is completely reduced.

Mix the vinegar, oil, mustard and agave syrup to a vinaigrette. Please season to taste! Season with salt and pepper from the mill.

On 4 deep plates first the iceberg lettuce, then pepper strips, the corn and the cocktail tomatoes distribute, as Topping now the warm mushrooms arrange. Drizzle the vinaigrette over it and sprinkle everything with the fresh herbs at the end.

Baba Ganoush

Ingredients

2 eggplants, approx. 500g, 3 tbsp sesame paste, (tahini), 3 tbsp lemon juice, 2 tbsp olive oil, 2 cloves of garlic, ½ bunch of smooth parsley, 1 tbsp black olives without stone, salt and pepper

Preparation

Preheat the oven to 220°C, wash the eggplants and prick a few times with a sharp knife.

Bake the aubergines until they are soft, and the skin is almost black. Then take them out of the oven and let them cool down a little.

Cut the still lukewarm aubergines in half and remove the soft flesh from the skin with a spoon.

Mix the pulp with the sesame paste, the lemon juice and the olive oil in a mixer.

Peel the garlic, press through the garlic press and add to the aubergine puree and season with salt and pepper.

Pluck the parsley leaves, chop the olives finely and sprinkle on the Baba Ganoush shortly before serving.

Tip: Goes wonderfully with pita bread.

Fun Fact

Baba Ghanoush is a puree of Arabic cuisine made from eggplants and sesame paste, which is served as a dip or side dish, e.g. with schawarma and falafel.

Lentil-Tomato-Salad

Ingredients

150 g red lentils, 500 ml vegetable broth, 1 lemon, the juice thereof, 3 tablespoons olive oil, 1 onion, finely chopped, 1 clove of garlic, 4 tomatoes, 1 box cress, sea salt and pepper

Preparation

Cook the red lentils in the vegetable stock for about 5 minutes until al dente. Then drain.

Mix lemon juice and olive oil, season with sea salt and pepper, add garlic. Cut the tomatoes into slices. Mix the lentils, the chopped onion, the tomatoes and the cress with the dressing.

Tip: The salad can be served lukewarm or cold.

Antipasti

Ingredients

3 large red peppers, 40 g toast, 2 tsp vinegar (white wine vinegar), 1 clove of garlic, 1 bunch of smooth parsley, 25 g pitted green olives, 10 tbsp olive oil, 3 small courgettes, 1 eggplant, 3 tbsp basil, finely chopped, lemon juice, balsamic vinegar

Preparation

Quarter the peppers and remove the seeds. Bake in the oven at 220° for approx. 20 - 25 minutes until the skin blisters. Then take it out and let it cool down a little and then skin it.

Dice toast bread, drizzle with vinegar and 1 tablespoon lemon juice.

Peel garlic, wash parsley leaves and pat dry.

Toast bread, garlic and parsley, puree the olives and 1 tablespoon olive oil in a blender, season with salt and pepper. Coat the pepper quarters with the paste and roll them up.

Wash the Aubergines and courgettes, cut the Aubergines crosswise and the courgettes lengthwise into slices. Fry the slices in portions in a pan in 1-2 tablespoons of olive oil on both sides until brown. Season with salt, pepper, balsamic vinegar and basil.

Tip: Serve with baguette.

Fun Fact

Antipasto (Italian for before the meal, plural antipasti) is the Italian term for appetizer. The antipasti of the

Italian cuisine consist of small dishes as a prelude to a multi-course menu. Typical are air-dried cold cuts such as ham or salami, accompanied by fried vegetables marinated in olive oil such as eggplants, courgettes, peppers, mushrooms or fresh vegetables or fruit, marinated fish and seafood as well as spicy toasted slices of bread.

Hot Carrot Salad with Herbs

Ingredients

750 g carrots, 1 large onion, 5 cloves garlic, 6 tablespoons olive oil, 4 lemons, including juice, 1 chilli pepper, 6 sprigs basil, 6 sprigs smooth parsley, 1 teaspoon smoked paprika powder, sea salt, black pepper

Preparation

Peel the carrots and plane them into 1mm thin slices. Peel onion and garlic and dice finely.

Squeeze out 3 lemons (you will need the 4th lemon later) and prepare 100 ml of water.

Dice the onion and sauté in 3 tablespoons of olive oil. Add the garlic and carrots. Sauté briefly, stirring. Add the water and lemon juice and simmer at low heat for 10 minutes. Stir frequently.

Now remove the seeds from the chillies and dice finely. Chop the parsley and basil finely.

Squeeze out the fourth lemon. Add salt, pepper, sugar and smoked paprika to the lemon juice and mix. Stir in the remaining 3 tablespoons of olive oil.

The carrots are now cooked, but should still be firm to the bite. After cooking, put the carrots in a bowl and mix in the chopped chilli and herbs.

Mix with the vinaigrette. If necessary, season to taste with the spices. It should taste sour and spicy.

Allow to stand for at least 2 hours.

Tip: Do not store the finished dish in the refrigerator, but in a cool place. Otherwise it will lose its aroma.

Tomatoes - Olive Relish

Ingredients

100 g red onions, 350 g tomatoes, 20 g brown sugar, 80 ml white balsamic vinegar, 80 g pitted Kalamata olives, 50 g snow peas, black pepper, sea salt (coarse), paprika powder

Preparation

Cut them onions and tomatoes into ½ cm cubes.

Cut the sugar snap peas lengthwise into fine strips.

Cut the Kalamata olives lengthwise in half and remove the stone.

Heat a pot with olive oil and sweat the onions with the mangetout briefly and vigorously. Now add the tomatoes. Deglaze with the balsamic vinegar.

Add the olives and season with sugar, pepper, sea salt and some paprika powder.

Hot Melon Skewers

Ingredients

½ Honey melon, ¼ Watermelon, 1 tbsp chopped oregano, ½ TL chilli flakes, 1 tsp ground (cumin) cumin, ½ TL chopped fennel seeds, ½ TL brown sugar, ½ TL salt, 1 tsp abrasion of an orange

Preparation

Core and peel the melon and cut it into large cubes.

Place the cubes alternately on skewers. You can also use honeydew melons of different colours with the watermelon to add some colour.

Finely chop the oregano and the orange zest (abrasion of the orange) and mix with the spices. Sprinkle on the melon skewers.

Sushi with Tofu

Ingredients

300 g tofu, 200 g spiced tofu, 200 g rice (Arborio), 100 g pickled bamboo shoots, 400 ml water, 200 ml rice vinegar, 10 pieces nori leaves, 4 tablespoons soy sauce, 4 tablespoons sunflowers

Preparation

Cut the tofu into long slices and fry in a pan with oil and soy sauce. Leave to cool.

Heat the seasoned tofu briefly in the same pan.

Simmer the rice with the water until the water is absorbed. This takes about 15 minutes.

Spread the rice on the algae so that about 3/4 of the leaf is covered.

Put in the tofu and bamboo shoots. Roll up the algae leaves using a mat or kitchen towel. Brush the last quarter with rice vinegar and stick the roll on.

Cut each roll into 5 pieces.

Roasted Peppers

Ingredients

4 yellow peppers, oil, for frying, salt, vinegar

Preparation

Wash all the peppers. And because it's so nice, now dab dry again.

Heat the oil in a high pan and add the peppers, sprinkle with salt and fry lightly on all sides. Cover the pan and sauté the peppers. Turn over frequently.

Then arrange in a bowl, add some of the oil and season with vinegar to taste.

Tip: Also suitable as a side dish.

Beetroot fried with Walnuts and Salad

Ingredients

500 large raw beetroot, 4 tbsp sunflowers, 4 tbsp balsamic vinegar, 100 g lamb's lettuce, 1 tbsp walnut oil, 50 g walnuts, salt and pepper, freshly ground

Preparation

Peel the beetroot and cut it into 1/2 cm thin slices.

Heat the sunflower oil slightly in a pan and fry the beetroot slices for a few minutes, turning once.

Dab the slices on kitchen paper, layer them in a bowl and season each layer with salt, pepper and balsamic vinegar.

Allow to stand in the fridge for a few hours.

Serve:

Wash and dry the green salad.

Drain the beetroot slices in a sieve, collecting the liquid.

Arrange the salad leaves and beetroot on plates. Mix the collected beetroot liquid with the walnut oil, season and drizzle over the salad and beetroot. Coarsely chop the walnut kernels and sprinkle over them.

Marinated Asparagus - Strawberry - Salad

Ingredients

250 g white asparagus, 250 g green asparagus, 250 g strawberries, 1 head of lettuce, 30 g pine nuts, 1 box of cress, 2 tbsp white balsamic vinegar, 1 tbsp sherry vinegar, 3 tbsp rapeseed or safflower oil, 1 tbsp walnut or pine nut oil, 1 tbsp icing sugar, salt and pepper, ground, some vegetable broth

Preparation

Peel and wash the asparagus. Cut the asparagus diagonally into bite-sized pieces. Then cook the white asparagus in salted water for 12-15 minutes until al dente.

Lightly caramelise the icing sugar in a frying pan, then toss the green asparagus pieces into it and pour in a little vegetable stock. Cook for 5 minutes until al dente. Drain both varieties well.

Mix a dressing with the sherry vinegar, balsamic vinegar, rapeseed or safflower oil, walnut or pine nut oil, salt and pepper and add the first half of cress. Add the asparagus to the sauce and marinate.

Wash and dry the salad and plate. Clean and halve the strawberries and spread them on the salad.

Fry the pine nuts in a pan without fat. Caution: At a certain moment, they burn very quickly. Always observe and stir the pine nuts.

Spread the asparagus on the salad, drizzle the rest of the dressing on the salad and strawberries and sprinkle with the second half of cress and the pine nuts.

Avocado - Tatar

Ingredients

2 tablespoons lemon juice, 1 teaspoon olive oil, 1 red onion, 20 g fresh ginger, 1 ripe avocado, 2 tablespoons water, 1 tablespoon coriander green, salt, pepper and sugar

Preparation

Whisk lemon juice, water and 1-2 tsp olive oil.

Finely dice the onion and ginger and mix into the marinade. Season with salt, pepper and sugar.

Peel and halve the avocado, remove the stone and dice the flesh. Carefully fold into the dressing and season to taste.

Sprinkle with 1 tablespoon chopped coriander green.

Tip: Fresh baguette or pumpernickel goes well with this.

Zucchini - Tomatoes - Vegetables

Ingredients

1 garlic clove, 3 tbsp olive oil, 600 g courgettes, 3 tomatoes, 1 tbsp tomato paste if required, 5 leaves basil, salt and pepper, dried oregano

Preparation

Wash the courgettes and cut them into 1 cm cubes. Lightly fry the courgette cubes in hot olive oil.

Slice the tomatoes crosswise and pour very hot water over them. Leave to stand for a short time, then skin and dice.

Peel the garlic clove, press and add to the courgettes. Add the tomato cubes.

Season with salt, pepper and oregano and stew for 5-8 minutes. If necessary, add some tomato paste and serve sprinkled with basil leaves as required.

Falafel

Ingredients

200 g dried chickpeas, 1 slice toast, 1 onion, 4 garlic cloves, ½ bunch parsley, 2 teaspoons ground coriander, 2 teaspoons ground cumin, 1 teaspoon baking powder, 1 litre oil to fry, 1 lemon, 2 tablespoons flour, salt and pepper

Preparation

Cover the chickpeas in a bowl with cold water and leave to soak for 12 hours. Then drain. Crumble the toast bread.

Peel onion and garlic and chop coarsely.

Wash the parsley and pluck the leaves.

Finely chop the bread, onion, garlic, parsley and chickpeas in a mixer.

Season the puree with coriander, cumin, pepper and salt and knead with the flour and baking powder. Form walnut-sized balls from the dough.

Heat the oil to fry. **Tip**: It is hot enough when many bubbles rise from a wooden spoon handle that you hold in the fat.

Fry the falafel in it in portions for 4-5 minutes until golden brown.

Drain on a thick layer of kitchen paper.

Tip: Cut the lemon into slices and serve with the hot falafel. Ready!

Fun Fact

Falafel are deep-fried balls made from pureed beans or chickpeas, herbs and spices, which are particularly popular as a snack. The dish comes from Arab cuisine.

Pumpkin Salad

Ingredients

400 g pumpkin (e.g. hokkaido, nutmeg pumpkin), 4 gherkins, 3 tomatoes, 3 tbsp herb vinegar, 4 tbsp oil, 1 onion, salt, sugar, chives

Preparation

Peel the pumpkin and grate it into fine strips.

Cut the gherkins, onion and tomatoes into small cubes and put everything in a bowl.

Prepare a sauce with vinegar, oil, salt and sugar and pour over the salad.

Chop the chives and sprinkle over them. Mix everything well and leave to stand for at least 6-8 hours in a cool place.

Carrots - Apple - Salad with Orange Dressing and Walnuts

Ingredients

500 g carrots, 1 large red apple, 4 tbsp walnuts

For the dressing:

5 tablespoons oil, 3 tablespoons vinegar, 1 orange, 1 cm fresh ginger, some salt and pepper

Preparation

For the dressing, squeeze the orange in a large bowl. Grate and add the ginger.

Add oil, vinegar, salt and pepper and mix well.

Peel the carrots. Wash, peel and seed the apple.

Grate the carrots and apple directly into a bowl. Mix everything together and leave in the fridge for 30 minutes.

Chop the walnuts coarsely and sprinkle over the salad when serving.

Carrot Salad with Peanuts

Ingredients

4 carrots, 1 tin peanuts, salted & roasted, 5 tbsp mango balsamic vinegar, 2 tbsp peanut oil

Preparation

Peel and finely grate the carrots. Add the peanuts.

Since the peanuts are already salty, season to taste carefully with salt and pepper.

Add the vinegar and the oil.

Bruschetta

Ingredients

4 spring or spring onions, 2 cloves of garlic, 1 pot of fresh oregano, 1 pot of fresh basil, 3 teaspoons vegetable oil, 8 tomatoes, 1 baguette stick

Preparation

Cut the tomatoes into pieces and place them in boiling water for a short time, then peel off the skin.

After removing the skin, the tomatoes are seeded and cut into small pieces.

Pluck the leaves from the basil and oregano bush and chop them into small pieces. Cut the spring onions and garlic into small pieces.

Put everything in a bowl and add the oil.

Season to taste with salt.

Cut the baguette into slices and fry in the pan with the oil until crispy.

Then cover the baguette with the salad. Serve immediately.

Fun Fact

Bruschetta belongs to the Italian antipasti. The original "poor people food" comes from central and southern Italy. Freshly roasted bread, such as Pane Pugliese (with hard crust), is rubbed warm with a halved clove of garlic and then drizzled with olive oil, peppered and salted as desired and eaten immediately. A topping with chopped tomatoes and fresh basil, for example, is common.

Rocket-Carrot and Mango Salad

Ingredients

125 g rocket salad, 2 carrots, ¾ ripe mangoes, possibly pine nuts, 3 tablespoons olive oil, 3 tablespoons light balsamic vinegar, some nutmeg, salt and pepper, salad herbs, freeze-dried or fresh

Preparation

Wash the rocket carefully in cold water and spin dry with a salad spinner.

Grate the carrots as finely as possible.

Cut the mango meat into small cubes.

Put the rocket, carrots and mango in a bowl.

Stir the oil, vinegar, spices and herbs into a dressing, pour over the colourful salad and mix well. Toast the pine nuts lightly in a frying pan and pour over the salad before serving. Caution: From a certain moment, they burn very quickly. Always observe and stir the pine nuts.

Taboulé

Ingredients

200 g fine-grained bulgur, 6 tomatoes, 1 cucumber, 4 spring onions, 1 handful freshly chopped parsley, 1 handful freshly chopped peppermint, 1 lemon, 2 tablespoons olive oil, salt and pepper

Preparation

Pour boiling water over the tomatoes, skin and cut into small cubes.

Peel the cucumber, remove seeds and cut into small cubes.

Cut the spring onion into thin slices.

Mix the above vegetables with the parsley and mint.

Add lemon juice and olive oil.

Mix everything and season with salt and pepper.

Add the bulgur.

Cool for four hours and let simmer. Stir well 2-3 times in between.

Fun Fact

Taboulé is a salad from Lebanese cuisine. It is served as a starter or snack, sometimes as a side dish on the table and can also be offered as a main course. In German-speaking countries it is called Bulgur salad. The Turkish variant is called Kısır (Kisir).

Piquant pickled dried Tomatoes

Ingredients

400 g dried tomato without oil, 1 bunch basil, 1 bunch parsley, 2 tbsp capers in brine, 1 tbsp sweet paprika powder, 1 tsp hot chilli powder, 1 tsp heaped turmeric, 2 cloves garlic, 1 dash vinegar, 200 ml olive oil, screw jars or preserving jars

Preparation

Taste the tomatoes first. If the tomatoes are already very salty, then put them in water at room temperature for 20 - 30 minutes and rinse well.

Put the tomatoes in a saucepan, cover them with water and add a dash of vinegar. Bring to the boil and cook for two minutes. Pour into a sieve and drain well.

Pluck the basil leaves from the stems and chop the parsley finely.

Drain the capers and chop coarsely.

Peel the garlic cloves and cut into wafer-thin slices.

Put the tomatoes, herbs, capers and garlic in a bowl and mix well together with the paprika, chilli and turmeric powder.

Place the tomatoes flat in glasses and squeeze gently. Fill with olive oil so that the tomatoes are covered. Screw the glasses together.

Leave to stand for about a week. Ready!

Tip: The oil is ideal for salad dressings.

Pea Salad with Avocado and Mint

Ingredients

500 g fresh peas, 1 avocado, 5 leaves fresh mint, 1 dash fresh lemon juice, salt and pepper, olive oil

Preparation

Steam or steam the peas until al dente. Then allow to cool.

Peel the avocado and cut into cubes.

Put the peas and avocado in a bowl.

Add pepper, salt, olive oil, lemon juice and finely chopped mint and mix carefully.

Avocado - Salsa with jacket Potatoes

Ingredients

8 firm boiling potatoes, 2 ripe avocados, 1 juice of a lemon, 1 shallot, ½ green chilli pepper or some cayenne pepper, 1 ripe tomato, 2 sprigs coriander green, smooth parsley, some chives, salt and pepper, saltwater

Preparation

Boil the potatoes in salted water. Depending on the taste, the skin can remain on the potatoes or not.

Peel the avocados and crush them with a fork.

Cut the shallot and tomato into small cubes. Cut the chilli and herbs into small pieces.

Mix everything together and season with salt, pepper and the juice of a lemon. Serve as a dip with the potatoes.

Tip: Avocadosalsa also tastes good as a spread on bread.

Baked Tofu

Ingredients

250 g Japanese tofu, 100 g wheat flour, 2 tbsp oil, 100 g Daikon radish (Japanese radish), 1-piece fresh ginger, Japanese soy sauce

Preparation

Immerse the tofu briefly in cold water. Drain, pluck thoroughly and carefully cut into 8 cubes of equal size.

Turn the tofu pieces in flour and bake in hot oil in a pan on each side for about 1 minute at medium heat until golden brown.

Peel radish and ginger and grate separately. Squeeze out the radish and form four equal portions by hand.

Arrange 2 pieces of tofu on each plate. Place a portion of radish next to each one and decorate with ginger on top. Add a small bowl of Japanese soy sauce.

Mediterranean Courgettes

Ingredients

1 medium zucchini, 2 cloves of garlic, 1 lemon, salt, pepper, sweet paprika powder, olives and (possibly) frozen herbs (8 herbs)

Preparation

Cut the courgettes into thick slices and put them in a bowl.

Squeeze the lemon and pour over the courgettes. Peel and press the garlic cloves or cut them into small cubes and add some olive oil. Season with salt, pepper and paprika powder.

Add herbs according to taste. Mix well and leave to stand for about 1 hour.

Fry the zucchini slices on the grill or in a pan.

Italian cucumber Salad

Ingredients

1 cucumber, 2 large meat tomatoes, 2 spring onions, 1 basil shrub, pepper & salt, oil

Preparation

Peel the cucumber, cut it into thin slices, sprinkle with salt and leave to stand for about half an hour.

Drain the liquid from the cucumber. Place the cucumber on a plate.

Cut the tomatoes into eighths and place them around the cucumber slices.

Place thin onion slices on top.

Season the tomatoes with pepper and salt. Pour over the whole oil and sprinkle with the chopped basil.

Fried Garlic - Fennel

Ingredients

1 tuber fennel, 1 tablespoon olive oil, 1 clove of garlic, salt and pepper

Preparation

Clean the fennel tuber. Cut the fennel tuber in half and cut it into fine strips. Put the fennel green aside.

Fry the fennel strips in hot olive oil with the garlic clove pressed through. Season with salt and pepper and serve with the chopped green leaves.

Tip: Tastes hot, lukewarm, cold and as a starter but also with noodles.

Potato Salad with Apples and Lentils

Ingredients

600 ml vegetable broth, 1 kg potato, 150 g lentils, 2 apples, 1 bunch leek onion, 8 tbsp neutral oil, 4 tbsp apple vinegar, 1 tsp sugar, salt and pepper

Preparation

Bring half of the vegetable stock to the boil and add the lentils. Cook on a low heat for 25-30 minutes.

Peel and slice the potatoes, then boil in salted water.

Drain the lentils through a sieve.

Clean the spring onions, cut into thin rings and fry in hot oil until translucent.

Add the rest of the stock and bring to the boil, then stir in the vinegar. Bring to the boil and remove from the heat.

Add the potato slices and mix in the lentils. Allow to simmer for 30 minutes.

Cut the unpeeled apple into thin slices and mix immediately with the potatoes and lentils and season with salt and pepper.

Mercimek Köftesi

Ingredients

1 glass extra fine Bulgar, ½ Glass red lentils, 2 onions, 4 spring onions, 2 handful smooth parsley, 5 tablespoons olive oil, 2 tablespoons sweet paprika powder, 1 teaspoon black pepper, 3 tablespoons salt, 2 tablespoons tomato or paprika puree, 1 tablespoon coriander powder, 1 tablespoon fresh mint, some lemon juice

Preparation

Cook the lentils for about 30 minutes in a very large pot. Make sure that the water is always 2 finger's width above the lentils.

Now add the bulgur and mix well. Put the lid on it and let it rest for 15 minutes.

In the meantime, cut the onions into small pieces and caramelise them in a frying pan.

Cut the spring onions and parsley into small pieces and put them aside.

In a small bowl mix the oil with the tomato paste and the spices. Then knead the mixture well into the lentil bulgur mixture.

Knead with your hands until the mixture is even. Finally add the onions, spring onions and parsley. Form golf ball sized balls and decorate best on salad leaves.

Fun Fact

Mercimek Köftesi comes from Turkey and is an appetizer made from lentils (Mercimek) in the form of elongated balls served on a salad leaf and drizzled with lemon juice shortly before consumption.

Buckwheat - Carrots - Bratlings

Ingredients

170 g buckwheat, 2 cups water, 300 g carrots, 200 g tofu, natural, 2 cl Tamari soy sauce, 2 tsp chili powder, 5 grains ground pepper, 150 g ground buckwheat, 4 cl Tamari soy sauce, olive oil for frying

Preparation

Wash buckwheat. Put the buckwheat in 2 cups of boiling water and bring to the boil. Lower the heat shortly after boiling.

When the water is below the buckwheat surface, turn off the heat. Put the lid on and let the buckwheat swell for 10-15 minutes. It now becomes dry and grainy.

Grate the carrots finely. Cut the tofu into small pieces, sprinkle with 2 teaspoons of chilli powder and let rest with 2 cl Tamari for about 20 minutes. Then puree.

Mix all Ingredients (except the olive oil) together, form into a roast, possibly spread a little tamari over it and leave to stand for about 10 minutes.

Form small bratlings with wet hands and fry in oil at medium heat from both sides.

Fruity Bean Salad with Thyme

Ingredients

1 tin of white beans, 1 apple, 1 orange, 1 m. large red onion, 2 tbsp fresh or chopped thyme, 4 tbsp germ oil or sunflower oil, 1 1/2 tbsp white wine vinegar, 3 tsp mustard, some salt and pepper

Preparation

Wash the white beans with lukewarm water, drain and place in a salad bowl.

Cut the apple into small pieces, fillet the orange and cut into small pieces.

Cut the red onion into cubes and put everything together with the thyme in the salad bowl and mix.

Mix the salad dressing in a separate bowl.

Mix oil, vinegar, mustard, salt and pepper to a smooth sauce with a whisk and then pour over the salad. Stir well and leave to stand for 1 hour.

Potato Salad

Ingredients

3 potatoes (approx. 350 g), 1/2 cup vegetable broth, 1 small onion, 1/2 tbsp margarine, 4 tbsp vinegar, 1/3 soymilk or vegetable broth, 1-2 tsp caraway, parsley or chives (optional), pepper and salt

Preparation

Boil the potato in its skin. Peel the potatoes and cut into very thin slices.

Mix soymilk (or vegetable stock) and vinegar and add to the potatoes with the caraway seeds.

Peel onion, dice finely and fry with margarine until translucent.

Deglaze with the vegetable stock, pour over the potatoes, fold in carefully.

Season with salt and pepper.

Allow to cool, leave to stand in the fridge for at least an hour.

Add parsley or chive rolls to taste.

Avocado Relish

Ingredients

2 ripe avocados, 1 untreated lemon or lime, 1 clove of garlic, 150 g cocktail tomatoes, 2 tbsp olive oil, 1/2 bunch smooth parsley or coriander, sea salt and black pepper

Preparation

Rub the lemon zest into a small bowl. Peel the garlic, press and add to the lemon peel. Press the lemon and add the lemon juice.

Chop the parsley into fine strips and add. Peel the avocados, cut into small cubes and add. Cut the tomatoes into cubes of about the same size and add them.

Sprinkle with a little olive oil, mix well and season with sea salt and pepper.

Let simmer a little. Ready!

Fun Fact

The avocado fruit, actually a berry, is pear-shaped to oval, depending on the species its leathery outer shell is medium to dark green (which has earned it the name alligator pear); inside there is a core about the size of a golf ball. The flesh is greenish yellow to golden yellow and oxidises to a dark colour when exposed to air - this can be prevented by rapid addition of antioxidants such as ascorbic acid contained in lemon juice. Certain varieties are also used for medicinal purposes (for example as a bactericide and against diarrhoea, or for controlled weight gain due to the high fat content of about 25%).

Lebanese Spinach - Particles

Ingredients

For the dough:

500 g flour, 250 ml lukewarm water, 100 ml oil, 1 teaspoon sugar, 1 teaspoon salt, ½ cubes fresh yeast, 1 pck dry yeast

For the stuffing:

500 g spinach, 2 m. large onions, 50 ml oil, ½ TL sumac, lemon juice, salt and pepper

Preparation

Put all the Ingredients for the dough in a bowl.

Knead the dough until it becomes smooth. Put some oil on the surface of the dough.

Cover the dough with cling film and 1-2 thick towels and put the dough aside for about 25 minutes.

Prepare the filling in between by washing the fresh spinach and cutting it into small pieces.

Cut the onions into small pieces and add to the spinach.

Sprinkle salt over the spinach and knead the spinach with the onions until a juice is obtained.

Pour the juice away. Then taste with lemon juice, oil, pepper, salt and sumac and knead a little further.

If you don't have sumac, you can do without it.

Roll out the dough and cut out circles about the size of a saucer.

Place the spinach filling in the middle of each dough and press a little. Grasp the edge of each circle at 3 points at the same distance between thumb and index finger and press together to form a triangle and a small edge from which the filling cannot run out.

Place the particles on a baking tray lined with baking paper and bake in a preheated oven at 200°C for 20-25 minutes until they are golden brown.

Tip: You can eat the particles cold or freeze them in advance.

Radish salad

Ingredients

3 bunch radishes, 1/2 tablespoon salt, 1 tablespoon sugar, 4 tablespoons balsamic vinegar, 1 tablespoon sesame oil, 1 tablespoon olive oil, 1 tablespoon neutral oil, 1/2 tablespoon soy sauce, 2 spring onions, ground pepper

Preparation

Wash and dry the radishes well.

Retain approx. 3 tbsp. of the tender inner leaves, wash again and dry well.

Lightly crush the radishes with a flat object. If the radishes are too thick, cut them lightly beforehand.

Sprinkle the radishes with salt and sugar and mix well in a bowl. Marinate for 30 minutes and drain.

Collect 4 tablespoons of the juice. Mix this juice with balsamic vinegar, soy sauce, all kinds of oil and pepper.

Let the radishes infuse the vinaigrette for at least 5 minutes. Meanwhile chop the radish green finely and cut the spring onions into rings. Mix both with the radishes and serve.

Aromatic Spinach Balls

Ingredients

1 kg leaf spinach, 2 - 4 garlic cloves, ½ - 1 fresh pepperoni, 5 tbsp olive oil, 1 dash lemon juice, 1 lemon for garnishing, crystal salt

Preparation

Wash the spinach, do not dry it, but put it wet in a pot and sprinkle it with some salt. Cover and let it collapse over medium heat for about 5 minutes. Rinse with cold water and drain in a sieve.

Peel the garlic and chop into small pieces.

Remove the seeds from the peppers and cut them very finely. Mix both well with lemon and oil.

Season the squeezed spinach (you can leave it as a whole or chop it roughly) with a little sauce, form it into balls and sprinkle with the rest of the sauce.

Zucchini Meatballs

Ingredients

500 g small zucchini, 100 g wholemeal wheat flour, 6 cloves of garlic, 1 teaspoon sea salt, 2 tablespoons parsley

Preparation

Grate the zucchini with the skin finely into a large bowl, add the remaining Ingredients and stir well until everything is bound.

Leave to swell for about 10 minutes.

Lightly heat the oil and fry the dough in small portions. Be careful when turning the dough, because it is quite wet.

Tip: If the dough has become too soft, you can add a wholemeal roll soaked in soymilk and squeezed out, the meatballs will taste looser. You can also coat the meatballs with breadcrumbs or roll them in sesame seed, everything improves the taste.

Pear and Cheese Salad

Ingredients

3 large pears, 4-5 slices normal Wilmersburger (vegan cheese), 1 onion, 1 bunch chives, 1-2 tbsp grape vinegar, 1 tbsp rapeseed oil, 1 tbsp agave syrup, nuts of your choice, salt, pepper

Preparation

Wash and core the pears and cut them into small pieces.

Cut the cheese slices into small rectangles. Finely chop the onion and chives.

For the dressing, mix the onions, vinegar, oil and chives with the agave syrup and season with salt and pepper. Mix well and leave to stand for 20 minutes. Sprinkle with fresh chives and nuts of your choice.

Stuffed Pancakes with Spinach, Lentils and Quinoa

Ingredients

250 g flour, 500 ml water, 250 g deep-frozen spinach leaves, 1 onion, 6 large tomatoes, 100 g quinoa, 150 g red lentils, 3-4 vegan mushroom-cheese slices, herbs of Provence, garlic granules, salt and pepper

Preparation

For the spicy pancakes mix flour with water, herbs of Provence, salt and garlic granules to a smooth dough and fry in oil. Keep the pancakes warm in the oven.

For the filling, cook the quinoa and the red lentils according to the instructions on the packet. Chop the onion into small pieces and sauté in oil.

Add the deep-frozen spinach with a few tablespoons of water and stir until the spinach has disintegrated.

Cut the tomatoes into fine cubes and the cheese into small pieces. Now add the tomatoes, quinoa and lentils to the spinach and mix well. Simmer for about 5 minutes. Finally add the cheese.

Season to taste with salt, pepper and Provencal herbs.

To serve, put a few spoons of the filling on a pancake and roll it up.

If you like a small dip, stir some Alnatura paprika-nut spread with a few tablespoons of hot water and serve. The fast and healthy pancakes are ready.

Sweet Potato Tortilla

Ingredients

6-8 vegan wheat tortillas, 2 large sweet potatoes, 1 lime, 1 large onion, 1 red pepper, 1 yellow pepper, 1 small eggplant, 5-6 okra, 1 tin kidney beans, 1 small soy yoghurt, 50 g pine nuts, 1 bunch fresh coriander green, agave syrup or syrup, brown cane sugar

Preparation

Peel the sweet potatoes, cut into small pieces and cook until soft.

Cut the onions and peppers into strips. Onion naturally before peel.

Cut aubergines into small slices and okra peppers into pieces.

Finely chop the coriander green and squeeze out the lime.

Brown the eggplants and okra in olive oil for 3-4 minutes and put aside.

Brown the onions and add the pepper strips and fry for a short time.

Add aubergines and okra peppers and mix everything with 1-2 tablespoons brown cane sugar. Finally add kidney beans.

Drain the sweet potato water and mash with the potato masher, add the lime juice and brown sugar and mix everything.

Heat the oven to 160°. Heat the wheat flat cakes for a short moment in the oven.

Now add 1-2 tablespoons sweet mashed potatoes to each pancake. Add a little vegetable mixture, 1 teaspoon pine nuts, 1 teaspoon agave syrup as well as some soy yoghurt and fresh coriander and roll everything up as tightly as possible. Repeat with the rest of the tortillas.

Cut equal pieces from the rolls. Arrange them on a plate and serve.

Summer Rolls with Peanut Dip

Ingredients

1 block natural tofu, 2 carrots, 1 mango, 1 papaya, ½ cucumber, ½ bunch coriander, ½ bunch mint, 24 rice dough plates, 1-2 tablespoons peanuts, 50g glass noodles, peanut butter, soy sauce, coconut milk

Preparation

Cook the glass noodles according to the instructions on the packet and cut into approx. 5 cm long pieces. Peel the mango and papaya and cut them into fine strips. Peel the carrots and cucumber and cut into thin strips together with the tofu. Wash and chop the mint leaves and coriander.

Heat a large pot with water and remove from the heat.

Place 2 rice dough plates in the warm water for about 20 seconds until they become soft and papery.

Remove the rice pastry plates from the water, drain and place them exactly on top of each other. Now place the finely chopped Ingredients on the lower end, fold the sides and roll them into a roll. Make sure that the roll is rolled tightly so that it does not fall apart when you cut it.

Do the same with the remaining rice dough plates.

Then cut the rolls into thick slices and put them in the fridge.

Mix 2 tbsp peanut butter, 1-2 tbsp soy sauce and 2 tbsp coconut milk. Depending on the consistency, add some more water. Spread the peanuts on the dip.

Now serve the summer roll pieces together with the peanut dip. A sweet chili dip is also delicious. A fresh and healthy snack for warm summer evenings is ready, but it is also suitable as an appetizer.

Summer Salad with fresh Asparagus

Ingredients

500 g green asparagus, 2 small chicory, 200 g mixed pickle salad or wild herb salad, 1 pck fresh raspberries, ½ Fresh mint, 150 g walnut kernels, ½ glass mango apricots jam, 1 tablespoon vegan margarine, sugar, agave syrup, white vegan balsamic vinegar, olive oil, salt and pepper

Preparation

First cook the asparagus (do not peel it) until it is al dente and then cut it into 1-2 cm pieces.

Wash the chicory and cut into fine strips.

Wash and cut the plucked lettuce.

Carefully wash the raspberries, remove the mint leaves and chop into small pieces.

Melt some vegan margarine in a small pot and add 2-3 tablespoons sugar and 2-3 tablespoons mango apricot jam. Then add the walnut kernels and caramelise.

For the dressing, mix 1 tbsp mango apricot jam, a little white balsamic vinegar and olive oil with salt and pepper. Add some agave syrup so that the dressing is slightly sweet.

Mix all salad Ingredients with the dressing and decorate with a few mint leaves as desired.

Cheese

Ingredients

1 cup yeast flakes, 1 tablespoon wheat flour, 3 tablespoons corn starch, 1/2 cup oil, 3 cups water, 1/2 teaspoon garlic, 1 teaspoon mustard

Preparation

Place the corn starch, yeast flakes and wheat flour in a cold pan.

Add the water, stirring constantly.

Place the pan on the stove and wait until the mixture becomes creamy, stirring constantly. Bring to the boil briefly.

Add mustard, oil and garlic.

Waldorf Salad

Ingredients

50g chopped walnuts, 50g seedless grapes, 3 stalks celery, 4 tbsp natural yoghurt, 3 apples, 4 tbsp vegan mayonnaise, 2 tbsp lemon juice

Preparation

Chop the celery and apples into small pieces. It is recommended to cut the apples into cubes.

Put the apples in a bowl and add the lemon juice.

Then add the celery, nuts, grapes, yoghurt and mayonnaise.

Mix well and season with salt and pepper. Ready!

Fun Fact:

The Waldorf salad was created at the end of the 19th century in New York in the Hotel Waldorf, the forerunner of the Hotel Waldorf-Astoria, but still without walnuts. Today, the walnut version is one of the classics of the salad kitchen.

Vegan meat Salad

Ingredients

250 g smoked tofu, 150 g gherkins, 3 tbsp cucumber liquid, 2 tsp sugar, 300 g vegan mayonnaise, salt and pepper, paprika powder

Preparation

Cut the smoked tofu and gherkins into small narrow strips and place in a large bowl.

Stir the mayonnaise with the cucumber liquid until smooth, season to taste, add to the bowl and mix.

Allow to infuse for about 15 minutes.

Soups and Stews

Cream of Pumpkin Soup

Ingredients
2 Hokkaido pumpkins, 800 g carrots, 2 medium-sized potatoes, ¼ celeriac bulb, 1 ginger, approx. 5-7 cm, 2 small chilli peppers, 1 clove of garlic, 1 medium-sized onion, 1.2 l vegetable stock, 1 can coconut milk, 1 tsp curry powder, salt and pepper, nutmeg, oil

Preparation
Seed the pumpkins and chillies.

Peel carrots, potatoes, ginger, onions, celery and garlic. Cut everything into cubes and sauté briefly in a large pan with a little oil.

Season with curry powder and deglaze with the broth. Simmer at low heat for about 30 minutes.

When the vegetables are soft, puree with a magic wand. If the soup is too thick, add some vegetable stock. Season to taste with the spices and stir in the coconut milk.

Heat again and puree with a hand blender.

Ready!

Pumpkin Soup with Ginger and Coconut

Ingredients
600 g Hokkaido pumpkin, 1 fresh ginger, 1 onion, 1 can unsweetened coconut milk, 2 tsp red curry paste, 500 ml vegetable broth, 1 potato, possibly pumpkin seeds, possibly ginger, sliced

Preparation
Heat the cream of the coconut milk in the pot.

Cut the onions and ginger into small pieces and add to the pot with the curry paste. Sweat for 3 - 4 minutes.

Cut the pumpkin into small cubes and add with the and potatoes and stew for 3 minutes.

Deglaze with coconut milk and vegetable stock.

Cook the entire contents of the pot for approx. 30 minutes until soft, then puree and pass through a sieve. Serve!

Roasted pumpkin seeds on the soup and garnished with some fried ginger slices.

Of course, only those who like.

Lentil Potato Stew

Ingredients
1 kg potatoes, 100 g red lentils, 2 cans tomatoes, 2 peppers, 2 onions, 1 courgette, 4 carrots, 4 cloves of garlic, 500 ml vegetable stock, 50 g tomato paste, 20 g paprika cream, apple or mirabelle vinegar, paprika powder, sweet or hot, nutmeg, freshly grated, olive oil, black pepper, salt, fresh or dried salad herbs, chilli, sugar

Preparation
Prepare the lenses according to the package instructions and rinse them with cold water.

Peel and eighth the potatoes.

Peel the carrots and cut them into 1 cm thick pieces.

Cut the courgettes and peppers into 1 cm thick pieces as well.

Cut the onions into thin rings and chop the garlic finely.

Heat the olive oil in a large pan and add all the Ingredients. Mix with salt, a pinch of sugar and pepper.

Roast for approx. 4 minutes, stirring frequently.

Now deglaze the Ingredients in the pot with vegetable stock until all Ingredients are well covered. Let everything cook for about 10 - 15 minutes. The potatoes should still be slightly firm to the bite.

Remove the pot from the heat, add the lentils and thicken everything with tomato paste and paprika powder.

Add vinegar and season with salt, pepper and nutmeg. Fresh or freeze-dried herbs can also be added.

Allow to stand for 1 hour and reheat. Ready!

Tomato Soup

Ingredients
50 g rice, or noodles, 500 ml tomatoes, 100 ml vegetable stock, 1 pinch salt, 1 pinch pepper, 2 dashes rice milk or coconut milk, some chopped rosemary or parsley

Preparation
Boil rice or noodles in enough water.

Bring the tomatoes to the boil in a separate saucepan, add the vegetable stock and season to taste with salt and pepper.

To serve, pour into a bowl and add rice or noodles.

Serve according to taste with rosemary or parsley and a dash of rice or coconut milk.

Watermelons - Gazpacho

Ingredients
900 g watermelon, 2 tomatoes, 1 small red pepper, 1 small onion, 100 ml tomato juice, 2 tablespoons olive oil, 1 teaspoon pomegranate syrup, salt, pepper

Preparation
Remove the melon meat from the skin, core and cut into coarse cubes.

Remove the seeds from the peppers and tomatoes and cut into coarse cubes.

Finely dice the onion.

Put everything in a container and puree with olive oil and tomato juice.

Flavour with pomegranate syrup, salt and pepper.

Pass the mass through a sieve that is not too finely meshed.

Cold the Gazpacho for 2 - 3 hours.

Pour into glasses to serve!

Fun Fact
Gazpacho is a Spanish cold soup made from uncooked vegetables (today also with fruit). She's from Andalusia. The original soup dates back to the Moors and was a white garlic soup made from cucumbers, bread, garlic, olive oil, vinegar, salt and water. The Ingredients were crushed in a mortar. Tomatoes and peppers were first brought from America to Europe by Christopher Columbus and were not part of this soup until the 18th century.

Coconut Soup with Sweet Potatoes

Ingredients
1 sweet potatoes, 2 spring onions, 10 mushrooms, 8 cherry tomatoes, 300 ml vegan vegetable broth, 200 ml coconut milk, ½ TL lemon grass, ½ TL ginger, 1 lime, some salt, some coriander green

Preparation
Peel and chop the sweet potato.
Cut the spring onions into rings, halve the mushrooms and tomatoes.

Cook the sweet potato in the hot broth for 5 minutes. Add coconut milk, lemon grass, ginger, 1 tablespoon lime juice, tomatoes and mushrooms and simmer for another 5 minutes.

Add the spring onions and let simmer.

Season with salt and sprinkle with coriander.
Can now also be pureed on request.

Fun Fact
Sweet potatoes, the red-fleshed tubers, are best suited both in terms of their cooking properties and their aroma. Similar to potatoes, tubers are cooked, baked, deep-fried, gratinated or roasted when washed or peeled. The unpeeled Preparation in a microwave oven is also possible. The taste remains well preserved. It can also be cooked in the oven with a bowl.

Mango Carrot Soup

Ingredients
600 g carrots, 2 ripe mangos, 2 shallots, 1 walnut-sized ginger, ½ red chilli pepper, 1 teaspoon mild curry powder, 2 tablespoons neutral oil, ¾ litres vegetable stock, 200 g unsweetened coconut milk, salt and pepper, a little lime juice or lemon juice

Preparation
Wash, peel and slice the carrots.

Peel mangos, remove stone. Put some nice pieces of mango aside for the garnish, please dice the rest.

Peel and chop the shallots and ginger.

Slice open the chilli pepper, remove the seeds and light-coloured partitions, cut the flesh into fine rings.

Heat the oil in a pan and sauté the carrots, shallots, ginger and curry.

Add the stock, mango cubes and chilli rings. Cover and simmer for about 15 minutes at low heat.

Puree the soup, add the coconut milk and heat again.

Season to taste with salt, pepper and lime juice.

Garnish in soup cups or soup plates with the mango pieces and serve.

Red lentil Coconut Soup

Ingredients
1 onion, 1 clove of garlic, 1 celery stalk, 1 red pepper, 1 large carrot, 3 cm ginger root, 2 teaspoons mild curry powder, 175 g red lentils, 700 ml vegetable stock, 400 ml coconut milk, 2 tbsp lime juice, salt, cayenne pepper, Thai basil, oil

Preparation
Peel and chop the onions and garlic.

Wash and chop the paprika and celery.

Peel and chop the carrot and ginger.

Heat the oil in a pan and sauté the ginger, onion, garlic and curry powder for about 1 minute.

Wash the lentils in a sieve, drain and add them to the ginger, onion, garlic and curry powder together with the paprika, celery and carrot.

Add vegetable stock and coconut milk and bring to the boil. Simmer for about 20-25 minutes until the lentils disintegrate and the vegetables are soft.

Puree the soup and strain through a sieve.

Season the soup with lime juice, salt and cayenne pepper and add the finely chopped Thai basil.

Fine Ginger and Carrot Soup

Ingredients
700 g carrots, 2 medium-sized onions, 2 tablespoons olive oil, 3/4 litres water, 1/4 litre freshly squeezed orange juice, 1 teaspoon fresh ginger, 2 teaspoons vegan vegetable stock, 1 teaspoon curry powder, smooth parsley, ground chilli, salt and pepper

Preparation
Peel and chop the carrots and onions.

Remove the rind from a teaspoon-sized piece of ginger and chop finely.

Heat the olive oil in a large pan and sauté the carrots, onions and fresh ginger, then add 1 teaspoon curry powder.

Add the water, orange juice and vegetable stock. Bring to the boil and then simmer covered for 15 minutes.

Now puree the soup finely.

Wash the parsley according to taste and cut into fine strips. Finally season the soup with salt, pepper and chilli and sprinkle with the parsley and serve.

Silesian Potato Soup

Ingredients
500 g potatoes, 500 g soup vegetables (carrots, root parsley, leek, celery), 1 litre vegetable broth, 2 tbsp oil, 1 onion, 50 ml soy cream, 1 bunch flat parsley, salt and pepper, thyme, marjoram

Preparation
Wash, peel and chop the potatoes and the soup vegetables. Then sauté briefly, add the vegetable stock and cook for approx. 20 - 30 minutes. Then puree.

Cut the onions into small cubes. Heat the oil and fry the onion in it until golden yellow.

Season the soup with salt, pepper, thyme and marjoram. Stir the onion and soy cream into the soup.

Serve the soup and sprinkle the parsley over the soup.

Almond - Broccoli - Soup

Ingredients
50 g ground almond, 625 g broccoli, 900 ml vegetable broth, 300 ml soymilk, salt and pepper

Preparation
Preheat the oven to 180 °C.

Sprinkle the almonds on a baking tray lined with baking paper.

Brown in the preheated oven for approx. 10 minutes. Put some of the almonds aside for the garnish.

Wash the broccoli and divide into small florets.

Steam the broccoli over boiling water for about 6-7 minutes.

Place the almonds, broccoli, broth and soymilk in a saucepan and puree with a blender. Season to taste with salt and pepper. Then reheat the puree. If the soup is too thick, broth can be added.

Pour into soup plates and garnish with the remaining almonds.

Sweet Potato-Banana Soup

Ingredients
400 g sweet potatoes, 400 g carrots, 1 bunch leek onions, 750 ml vegetable broth, 3 bananas, 1 tbsp grated ginger, 400 ml coconut milk, 1 tbsp aniseed, salt and pepper, chilli powder, curry powder, Garam masala, some mint stalks, a little oil

Preparation
Quarter the sweet potatoes and cook. Grate the carrots and chop the spring onions. Crush the bananas with a fork and grate the ginger. Cut the mint into small pieces and grind or mortar the anise seeds.

Heat the oil in a saucepan and sauté the grated carrots and spring onions briefly. Add the vegetable stock and simmer for 5 to 10 minutes.

Then skin the cooked sweet potatoes, cut into cubes and add the bananas, ginger and ground aniseed seeds to the sizzling pot.

Bring everything to the boil again briefly, take from the stove and puree. Gradually the coconut milk is added.

Season with salt, pepper, chilli, curry and Garam Masala and add chopped mint.

Bring to the boil again briefly and garnish with chopped mint or whole mint leaves before serving.

Fun Fact
The sweet taste of sweet potatoes is due to their high sugar content. In addition, the tuber mainly contains the so-called batata or sweet potato starch.

Broccoli Cream Soup

Ingredients
1 broccoli, 4 potatoes, 1 onion, 1 clove of garlic, 3-4 cups vegetable broth, ½ cup soymilk, 2 tablespoons margarine, salt

Preparation
Peel onions, potatoes and garlic.

Dice the potatoes, cut the onion into eighths and place in a saucepan with the garlic. Cover with vegetable stock.

Cook in a closed pot for 5 minutes.

Meanwhile, separate the broccoli florets and cut the stems into small pieces.

Add the broccoli and cook for another 15 minutes.

Add the soymilk and margarine and puree. Depending on the desired consistency, add a little vegetable stock.

Season to taste with salt and bring to the boil again.

Mushroom Cream Soup

Ingredients
150 g mushrooms, 1 small onion, 1 small potato, 1 tablespoon margarine, 1 tablespoon flour, 1 ½ cup vegetable stock, ½ cup soymilk, 2 tablespoons vinegar, 1 tablespoon lemon juice, pepper, parsley

Preparation
Peel the skin from the mushrooms, remove the lamellas and cut into slices.

Peel and dice the onion with 2/3 of the margarine and steam the mushrooms until translucent.

Stir in the flour.

Peel the potatoes, cut into very thin slices and add to the mixture.

Deglaze with vinegar and vegetable stock.

Now cook until the potatoes are done.

Puree the soup, add the soymilk and lemon juice and season to taste with pepper.

Remove from heat, add remaining margarine.

Sprinkle with chopped parsley. Ready!

Leek Soup

Ingredients
½ leek, 2 tbsp margarine, 2 tbsp wheat flour, 2 cups vegetable stock, 3-4 tbsp soymilk, 1 tbsp lemon juice

Preparation
Remove roots and outer leaves from leek, green end l.s.

and wash thoroughly.

Cut the leek into rings and sauté in margarine.

Stir in the flour until it has combined with the margarine.

Add the vegetable stock, soymilk and lemon juice and bring to the boil briefly.

Orange-Carrot Soup

Ingredients
2 oranges, 1 kg carrots, 45 g butter, 240 g onions, 2 tsp sugar, 1 stalk lemon grass, 1 tsp curry powder, 600 ml vegetable broth, 200 ml orange juice, 200 ml coconut milk, some salt, some cayenne pepper, some coriander green

Preparation
Completely remove the peel and white skin of the orange and cut into coarse cubes.

Peel carrots and cut into slices. Then chop the onion coarsely! Remove the outermost leaves from the lemongrass stick and cut into small pieces.

Melt the butter in a saucepan and sauté the onion a little. Add the sugar and caramelise lightly.

Add lemon grass and curry powder and sauté briefly.

Add the orange pulp and carrots and deglaze with the broth, orange juice and coconut milk.

Let simmer for about 20 minutes. The carrots should still be firm to the bite! Remove about 4 tablespoons of carrots and put aside, cook the soup for another 15 minutes.

Then puree the soup. Season with salt and cayenne pepper if necessary.

Now add the previously removed carrot pieces and arrange in plates. Garnish with freshly chopped coriander green to taste!

15 Minutes - Vegetables - Noodles - Soup

Ingredients
1400 ml vegetable bouillon, 100 g noodles, 1 small onion, 2 carrots, 1 courgette, 1 yellow pepper, 4 ripe tomatoes, some salt and pepper, some chives, finely chopped, some parsley, finely chopped, some oil

Preparation
Heat some oil in a saucepan. Peel and chop the onion and steam in hot oil for about 3 minutes.

Pour in the vegetable stock and bring to the boil.

In the meantime, peel the carrots, wash the courgettes and cut them into thin slices.

Wash and seed the peppers and cut into small cubes. Wash the tomatoes, remove the stems and chop coarsely.

Add carrot slices to the boiling broth and precook for about 2 minutes, then add courgettes and noodles and cook for about 8 - 10 minutes at medium heat until al dente.

After approx. 5 minutes add the pepper and tomato cubes and season with spices.

Arrange the soup in deep plates and garnish with finely chopped chives and parsley.

African Peanut Stew

Ingredients
½ White cabbage, 2 carrots, 2 tsp cayenne pepper, 1 tsp thyme, ½ tsp paprika powder, 1 tbsp mustard, 1 small tin kidney beans, 1 tin maize, 1 pepper, 4 tbsp peanut butter, 1 pck strained tomato, 250 ml vegetable stock, 1 tbsp cumin, 1 onion, some mango juice, some salt and pepper

Preparation
Wash, peel and chop the onions, pepper, carrots and cabbage.

Precook white cabbage and carrots separately in water, then put aside.

Meanwhile, fry the onion and pepper pieces in oil. Add cumin, cayenne pepper and mustard and fry briefly.

Add the puréed tomatoes and broth and cook for 5 minutes.

Add thyme, paprika powder and peanut butter. Stir well.

Drain kidney beans and corn, add and simmer again.

Season with mango juice, salt and pepper and possibly some cayenne pepper.

Tip: Best served with rice or noodles.

Creamy Beetroot - Carrots - Soup

Ingredients
400 g peeled beetroot, 300 g carrots, 1 m. large white onion, 2 tablespoons oil, 1 litre vegetable broth, 5 potatoes, 1 piece chopped celery, horseradish, fresh or out of the glass, white pepper and sea salt

Preparation
Wash the beetroot and the carrots and cut into small pieces.

Peel and chop the potatoes.

Peel and chop the onion.

Brown the onions in oil and add some celery. Add the finely chopped vegetables and sauté.

Add the vegetable stock and cook.

If you want, you can puree the soup. Season to taste with the spices.

Season to taste with horseradish. If you don't like horseradish, you can of course leave it out.

Curry - Ginger - Apple - Soup

Ingredients
500 ml naturally cloudy apple juice, 800 ml coconut milk, 8 tbsp mild curry powder, 10 cm ginger, 2 large potatoes, 3 tbsp vegetable stock

Preparation
Bring apple juice and coconut milk to the boil in a saucepan. Add the curry powder and vegetable stock and stir.

Peel the ginger, press through a garlic press and add to the soup.

Peel and chop the potatoes and add to the soup.

As soon as the potatoes have been softened, puree with a blender.

Potato Soup with Mushrooms

Ingredients
1 small onion, 250 g potatoes, 1 tsp vegetable oil, 250 ml vegetable broth, 100 g brown mushrooms, salt and pepper, nutmeg

Preparation
Cut onion and potatoes into small cubes. Heat the oil in a saucepan and sauté both in it until glassy.

Add the vegetable stock and simmer the soup covered for about 15 minutes.

Clean and slice the mushrooms.

Remove half of the soup, puree and return to the pot.

Add the mushrooms to the soup and cook for about 5 minutes.

Before serving, season the soup with salt, pepper and nutmeg.

Bananas - Coconut - Chili - Soup

Ingredients
2 spring onions, 1 garlic clove, 200 ml coconut milk, 400 ml vegetable broth, very ripe banana, 2 chilli peppers, 1 tablespoon oil, salt and pepper, sugar

Preparation
Cut the spring onion, garlic clove, chilli peppers (if two chilli peppers are too hot, they take less) and the banana into thin fine slices.

Heat the oil in a pan and sauté the spring onion, garlic and chilli peppers briefly.

Pour in coconut milk and vegetable stock, bring the soup to the boil and season with pepper, salt and sugar.

Let the soup simmer for 5 minutes. Then add the banana and puree the soup. Heat the soup again briefly and decorate with banana slices if necessary.

Lentil Soup

Ingredients
100 g red lentils, 5 tbsp tomato paste, 1 onion, 1 small clove of garlic, 700 ml water, 2 tsp instant vegetable broth, 125 g smoked tofu, 1 tbsp soy sauce, olive oil, lemon juice, some curry powder, cumin, pepper and salt, tabasco or chilli powder

Preparation
Cut the onion into small pieces and fry in a pan with olive oil until lightly browned.

Add tomato paste, finely chopped garlic and lentils. Fry everything together briefly and deglaze with the water.

Flavour with a little curry, cumin, pepper and a dash of lemon juice. Caution with cumin, this is very intense!

Sharpen with Tabasco or chilli powder to taste. Important: Add salt at the end, otherwise the lenses will not soften.

Bring to the boil and puree with a hand blender.

Let simmer for 10-15 minutes.

Meanwhile, cut the smoked tofu into small cubes and add at the end.

Flavour with instant vegetable stock and soy sauce.

Lemon Grass - Coconut Milk - Soup

Ingredients
1 tbsp vegetable oil, 1 litre water, 80 g coconut milk powder, 2 tsp instant vegetable stock, 1 tsp turmeric, 1-piece ginger, thumb-sized, 4 stalks lemongrass, 8 minimaiskolben, 1 handful sugar peas, 3 spring onions, a few splashes of lime juice

Preparation

Wash the minimaiskolben and cut into thirds.

Wash and chop the sugar snap peas.

Clean the spring onions and cut them into rings.

Peel the ginger and crush it in a mortar or chop it into very small pieces. Wash lemongrass and whip with a mortar or knife handle.

Heat the oil in a pan and sauté the vegetables including ginger briefly.

Add a few spritzers of lime juice and deglaze with 800 ml water. Bring to the boil.

Add bouillon powder and turmeric and cook for 5 minutes.

Dissolve coconut milk powder in remaining water and pour in. Let the soup simmer for 20 minutes at low heat.

Before serving, remove the lemongrass as they are too tough.

Zucchini - Coconut - Soup

Ingredients
800 g zucchini, 1 onion, 2 tbsp oil, 2 tsp green or yellow curry paste, 400 ml vegetable broth, 400 ml unsweetened coconut milk, ½ orange (zest), 1 bunch coriander green, 4 sprigs peppermint, 2 cloves garlic, salt and pepper

Preparation
Cut onions into small cubes and sauté in hot oil until translucent.

Add 2-4 teaspoons of green or yellow curry paste, depending on the desired spiciness. With yellow curry paste the soup becomes yellow instead of green!

Stir the zucchini and fry for 3 minutes.

Add vegetable stock and coconut milk, cover and bring to the boil, simmer at low heat for approx. 10 minutes.

Meanwhile, chop the garlic clove and coriander green into small pieces and mix with the orange zest and the chopped peppermint.

Puree the soup and season with salt and pepper. Serve with the herb mixture.

Semolina Soup with Vegetables

Ingredients
2 carrots, 1-piece celery, 1 leek, 1 tbsp oil, 2 tsp vegetable stock, salt and pepper, semolina (as desired)

Preparation
First peel, clean and finely plane the carrots and celery.

Cut the leek into small strips.

Heat the oil in a pan and add the vegetables and fry lightly. Then add the semolina (quantity as desired) and roast with it.

Add approx. 3/4 l water and season with vegetable boullion, salt and pepper.

Simmer at a low heat until the vegetables are soft.

Tofu - Soup

Ingredients
1.5 l vegetable stock, 100 g smoked tofu, 2 tbsp oil, 2 cloves of garlic, 200 g carrots, 150 g mushrooms, 1 bunch spring onion, 3 tbsp white wine, 3 tbsp soy sauce, 1 pinch ground ginger, 1 tsp agave syrup, 1 pinch chilli powder, 1 pinch grated lemon zest

Preparation
Heat the oil and brown the tofu.

Chop the garlic into small pieces, add and fry briefly.

Add the carrots (finely diced), mushrooms (very thin slices) and spring onions (cut thin rings) and stir-fry for 2-3 minutes.

Add the vegetables to the boiling vegetable stock.

Flavour with wine, soy sauce, agave syrup and spices.

Gazpacho

Ingredients
850 ml tomato juice, ½ medium cucumber, ½ green pepper, ½ red pepper, 6 slices vegan white bread, 3 tomatoes, 2 garlic cloves, 6 tbsp olive oil, 3 tbsp white wine vinegar, 1 red onion, ½ TL sugar, salt and pepper

Preparation
Finely chop the onions, tomatoes, cucumber and peppers and put them in a bowl with a clove of garlic.

Add tomato juice, sugar, salt and pepper as well as vinegar and oil. Stir well and keep cold.

Preheat the oven to 180°C.

Cut the white bread into approx. 1 cm cubes. Mix the oil and the second clove of garlic and drizzle over the diced white bread. Bake on a baking tray for approx. 10 minutes until golden brown. Turning now and then.

Tip: Serve the cold soup with the garlic croutons. Decorate the plate with basil leaves.

Fun Fact
Gazpacho is a Spanish cold soup made from uncooked vegetables (today also with fruit). She's from Andalusia. The original soup dates back to the Moors and was a white garlic soup made from cucumbers, bread, garlic, olive oil, vinegar, salt and water. The Ingredients were crushed in a mortar. Tomatoes and peppers were first brought from America to Europe by Christopher Columbus and were not part of this soup until the 18th century.

Tom Kha Hed Soup

Ingredients
150 g mushrooms, 150 g oyster mushrooms, 4-5 sticks lemon grass, 4 spring onions, 1 lime, 2 cans unsweetened coconut milk, 250 ml boletus yeast broth, 2 red chilli peppers, ½ bunch coriander leaves, approx. 10 cm galgant-root (also called Thai ginger), 8-10 Kaffir lime leaves, 1 teaspoon brown sugar

Preparation
Heat the boletus yeast broth with the coconut milk in a large pot.

Peel the galangal and slice it.

Cut the lemongrass stalks several times lengthwise, flatten them slightly with a knife and tie them into knots.

Put all 4-5 lemongrass stalks together with the kaffir lime leaves and the galgantscheiben in the pot and simmer for 10-15 minutes. Then strain the soup.

Meanwhile cut the mushrooms into fine slices.

Cut spring onions into fine rings. Core the chillies and cut into thin strips. Wash the coriander and pluck the leaves, squeeze the lime.

Now add the mushrooms and half of the chilli peppers and the lime juice to the soup.

Cook again for a few minutes, then season to taste with brown sugar. Finally, place the soup in a deep plate and arrange with the spring onion rings, coriander and the rest of the chilli strips. Ready!

Fun Fact
Tom Kha Hed soup is a Thai soup.

Baden-Style Stew

Ingredients
2 kg waxy potatoes, 100 g lentils, 1 kg ripe tomatoes, 2 peppers, 2 medium onions, 1 courgette, 3-4 carrots, 2 cloves fresh garlic, 20 g tomato puree, 1 bunch chives, apple vinegar, sweet paprika powder, whole nutmeg, olive oil, black pepper and salt, vegan instant vegetable stock

Preparation
Peel and eighth the potatoes.

Wash or peel the carrots thoroughly, then cut into 1 cm long pieces. Remove the stalk from the tomatoes and cut into eighths.

Cut the courgettes, peppers and carrots into 1 cm thick strips.

Cut the onions into thin rings and chop the garlic.

Put everything in a big pot or a pan. Add 4 tablespoons olive oil, salt, a pinch of sugar and freshly ground pepper and mix. Roast for 5 minutes at maximum heat, stirring often.

Prepare the lenses according to package instructions, drain into a sieve and rinse thoroughly with cold water.

Now add as much vegan instant vegetable stock as necessary until everything is just covered with liquid. Depending on the thickness of the potato pieces, cook for 10-15 minutes at medium heat.

When the potatoes are still slightly firm to the bite, remove from the heat.

Add the lentils to the vegetables and thicken with tomato paste.

Add 1 tbsp apple vinegar, season with salt, pepper and sweet paprika powder, refine with freshly grated nutmeg. If desired, finely chopped fresh herbs can be added.

If everything can be left to stand for an hour in a closed pot, it is of course ideal for the taste. Heat again, add some chives and you're done!

Pea Soup

Ingredients
1 tbsp oil, 1 onion, 1 bay leaf, 3 cloves of garlic, 400 g dried yellow or green peas, 75 g pearl barley, 1.5 tsp salt, 1.75 l water, 3 carrots, 3 celery stalks, 3 potatoes, 3-4 tbsp chopped fresh parsley, ½ tsp dried basil, ½ tsp dried thyme, ½ tsp mill pepper

Preparation
Place the oil in a large soup pot and heat at medium temperature.

Chop the onion into small cubes.

Brown the onions, bay leaf and garlic for 5 minutes while stirring until the onion is glassy.

Add the peas, pearl barley, salt and water and mix well.

Bring to the boil briefly, reduce the temperature and simmer for 2 hours, stirring several times.

When the 2 hours are over, add carrots, celery, potatoes, parsley, basil, thyme and pepper. Simmer for 1 hour until the peas and vegetables are soft.

Green Garden Soup

Ingredients
¼ l vegetable broth, 1 onion, 1 carrot, 2 celery sticks, 50 g long grain rice, 100 g fresh spinach, 2 small Romana salad heads, 6-8 tablespoons chopped fresh parsley, 1 pinch cayenne pepper, salt and pepper

Preparation
Chop onions into small pieces, wash carrots and celery and cut into thin slices.

Bring the vegetable stock, onion, carrot, celery and rice to the boil in a large pan and simmer covered for 30-35 minutes.

Meanwhile, pluck the salad and chop the parsley.

Put the spinach, salad and parsley in a separate pot. Cover with water and bring to the boil once, drain immediately and add to the soup the previously simmered 30-35 minutes.

Season with salt, pepper and cayenne pepper. Fine puree.

Add a little more broth to the soup if it's too thick. Serve immediately or cool overnight.

Vegetable Soup

Ingredients
1 medium white cabbage, 1 onion, 3 large carrots, 3 diced celery sticks, 3 tomatoes, 450 g frozen or fresh green beans, 2 bags onion soup, 1,75 l water

Preparation
Cut all vegetables into small pieces.

Put all Ingredients in a large soup pot, bring to the boil, reduce temperature and simmer for about 30 minutes until the vegetables are soft.

Who would like can puree the whole then also still.

Hearty Minestrone

Ingredients
1 l vegetable stock, 2 cans chopped tomatoes, 1 large potato, 1 onion, 2 celery sticks, 2 carrots, 1 large white cabbage, 4 tablespoons chopped fresh parsley, 4 tablespoons chopped fresh basil, 1 can kidney beans, 500 g frozen corn, 1 large courgette, 500 g star noodles, salt and pepper

Preparation
Wash all vegetables, peel if necessary and cut into small pieces.

Mix vegetable broth, tomatoes, potato, onion, celery, carrot, cabbage and herbs in a large soup pot. Bring to the boil, reduce heat and simmer for 15 minutes.

Stir in the corn, beans, courgettes and noodles and simmer for another 15 minutes until the vegetables and noodles are cooked.

Season with salt and pepper.

Fun Fact:
Minestrone is a nice vegetable soup from Italy. In the classic, northern Italian variant, it consists of various vegetables such as celery, carrots, leeks, peas, tomatoes and potatoes, as well as savoy cabbage and beans (borlotti).

Main Courses and Side Dishes

Vegan Tomato Quiche

Ingredients
For the dough
660 g wheat or wholemeal flour, 300 g margarine, 160 ml water, 1 teaspoon sea salt

For the filling
800 g silk tofu, 800 g cherry tomatoes, 4 tbsp olive oil, 4 tbsp cornflour, 2 tsp sea salt, 2 tsp turmeric, 2 pinches freshly grated nutmeg, 2 tsp fresh thyme, 2 tsp fresh oregano, 2 tbsp fresh chives, 6 tbsp fresh basil, freshly ground pepper

Preparation
For the quiche dough, process all dough Ingredients into a smooth dough and leave to rest in the refrigerator for 30 minutes covered.

Now wash the tomatoes for the filling, dry well, halve and put aside.

Puree the silk tofu with the oil, cornflour, salt and spices to a creamy mass.

Wash, dry and finely chop the fresh herbs and stir into the filling.

Roll out the dough on a large piece of baking paper to the size of your quiche tin + edge and slide into the quiche tin with the baking paper.

Press the dough against the mould and press the edge down firmly.

Pre-bake at 200°C top/bottom heat for 10 minutes. Then spread the filling on the dough and cover the filling with the halved tomatoes with the skin down (so the water in the tomatoes does not soften the quiche).

Bake the quiche at 200°C for a further 20 minutes and then reduce the temperature to 175°C. Bake the quiche for a further 15 minutes.

Tip: Leave the quiche to rest for about 10 minutes before slicing and then serve. It goes well with a small colourful salad.

Fun Fact

A quiche is a speciality of French cuisine, originally from the Lorraine region, which corresponds to the Preparation of a tart. It is a hearty short pastry baked in a round, flat shape with a spicy filling or coating. The French name "Quiche" was derived around 1845 from the Alsatian word "Kichel", which corresponds to the High German word "Kuchen". Quiches are baked in round tart moulds.

Creamy Peanut Pan with Vegetables and Soya

Ingredients
3/4 cup soy granules, 1 medium onion, 1 clove of garlic, ½ carrot, ½ courgette, 1 can corn, 100 ml strong vegetable broth, 150 ml soy milk, 3 tbsp soy sauce, 3 tbsp peanut butter, 1 tbsp parsley, some chili powder, some pepper, possibly curry powder, possibly paprika powder, some vegetable oil, for frying, possibly flour, for thickening, hot vegetable broth as required

Preparation
Put the soy granules in a bowl.

Bring the vegetable broth to the boil and pour over the granules, swelling well. It should not lie in the dry at least.

Leave to swell for 5 minutes. Then squeeze out properly and season with a little salt or broth if necessary.

Heat the vegetable oil in the pan and add the granules. You can achieve the best taste if you let the granulate stew well until it is browned and crispy.

Then add the diced onions, carrots and the crushed garlic clove and brown lightly.

Now add the diced courgettes and the corn.

Deglaze with a mixture of soymilk, vegetable stock and soy sauce.

Add the peanut butter, pepper and chilli powder.

Put the lid on and simmer until the zucchini is done. If it has become too thick, add a little soymilk or water.

Finally, season to taste again. The sauce should be creamy and with a good spiciness.

If you like, add some broth, salt, chili powder or pepper.

Tip: It goes well with rice. If you like, you can also choose other side dishes.

Vegan Bratwurst

Ingredients
600 g seitan flour, 60 g yeast flakes, 2 tsp garlic powder or garlic granulate, 4 msp cumin, 8 tsp paprika powder, 4 msp pepper, 6 tsp salt, 4 pinches sugar, 4 tsp onion powder, 12 tbsp oil, 2 tsp mustard, 8 tbsp soy sauce, 12 tbsp tomato puree, 700 ml water

Preparation
Place in a bowl Seitan flour, yeast flakes, garlic, cumin, paprika, salt, pepper and onion powder.

In a second bowl add oil, mustard, soy sauce, tomato paste and water.

Mix the Ingredients well in each bowl.

Pour the liquid Ingredients into the dry Ingredients and knead well.

Now form 10-12 sausages with a diameter of approx. 2 cm. Wrap the sausages first in baking paper and then firmly in aluminium foil.

Bake in the oven at 180°C for 50 minutes, then turn off the oven and leave the sausages in the oven for another 15 minutes.

Remove from oven and unwrap immediately.

Tip: The sausages taste cold, warm, fried or grilled and cut into soups.

Lasagna

Ingredients
400 g peeled tomato, 100 g tomato tofu, 1 tsp instant vegetable stock, ¼ tsp salt, ¼ tsp sugar, ¼ tsp paprika powder, ¼ tsp pepper, 350 ml tomato sauce, 250 g lasagne plates, ½ tsp yeast flakes, 1 tsp flour, ½ tsp margarine, ¼ tsp salt, ½ tsp mustard, 75 ml water

Preparation
Crush the peeled tomatoes and the tomato tofu with a fork in a bowl.

Add the vegetable stock, salt, pepper, paprika and sugar and stir.

Put some oil in a fireproof dish, layer the first layer of lasagne leaves and then alternate the sauce and noodles.

If the sauce is used up, simply continue to layer with the finished sauce from the glass. Finally apply a layer of lasagne sheets.

Preparation of the cheese:
Put yeast, flour, margarine, salt, mustard and water in a pot and heat while stirring until a light "processed cheese" has formed.

Remove from the heat and pour over the lasagna.

Now bake the lasagne for 30 minutes at 200°C on the lower rail without lid.

Fun Fact
According to a less widespread theory, there should be an English origin for the court: In the 14th century Forme of Cury, a collection of recipes prepared by chefs at the court of King Richard II of England, the dish "loseyns" (pronounced "lasan") is described,

which also contains layered pasta plates baked with cheese.

Millet - Scrambled Eggs

Ingredients
1 onion, 250 g tofu, ½ pepper, 2 mushrooms, salt and pepper, turmeric or curry powder, deep-frozen herbs, some vegetable oil

Preparation
Put some vegetable oil in a pan and heat.

While the pan is getting hot, crumble the tofu into it by hand (not too small). Fry the tofu until it is golden yellow.

In the meantime, chop the peppers, mushrooms and onion.

Now season the tofu with turmeric. This gives it its scrambled eggs-like colour. Add the vegetables and fry a little.

Season with salt and pepper and finally add the frozen herbs (e.g. chives and parsley).

Fun Fact
Millet is a collective name for small-fruited husk cereals with 10-12 genera. They belong to the family of sweet grasses (Poaceae). Millet is the grain richest in minerals. Millet contains fluorine, sulphur, phosphorus, magnesium, potassium and especially a lot of silicon (silicic acid) and iron. The golden millet, which is free of shells, is common in the trade. There is also the unpeeled brown millet, in which most of the minerals and trace elements adhering to the shells are preserved. However, the prussic acid content may not be completely harmless, especially in the case of raw millet.

Millet - Pan

Ingredients
100 g millet, 1 chilli pod, 1 tsp dill **Tip**s, ½ tsp turmeric, ¼ tsp nutmeg, 2 cloves garlic, approx. 1 tsp finely chopped ginger, ½ tsp turmeric, 2 small onions, ½ small courgettes, ½ leek stalk (without onion tuber), ¼ cup soy sauce, 1 ½ tbsp sesame oil, ½ tbsp fresh black pepper, 3 small brown mushrooms, 1 ½ small carrots, water if required

Preparation
Place the millet in a sieve and rinse well with hot water. Then pour into a coated pan and cover with plenty of water. Cook the millet until there is hardly any liquid left.

In the meantime, grate the carrots and courgettes. Clean and chop the mushrooms.

Finely chop the piece of ginger, chilli peppers, garlic, leek and the peeled onions. Pour the spices into a cup and mix well.

Repeatedly add about 2 cups of water to the millet, then stir in the vegetables and add about half of the spice mixture.

Add the sesame oil and the soy sauce and stir. Then add the rest of the seasoning mixture and stir well again.

There should still be enough liquid in the pan, otherwise add more water if necessary and cook on a low flame for about 20 to 25 minutes with the lid slightly open.

Tip: Serve the millet immediately or form it into a roast and sauté until golden brown.

Lemon-Fennel Risotto

Ingredients
100 g risotto, ½ tuber large fennel, ½ onion, ½ garlic clove, 75 ml white wine, 0.35 litre vegetable broth, 1 tablespoon olive oil, ½ organic lemon, grated peel and juice thereof, 1 tablespoon capers, ½ TL heaped white almond paste, ½ tablespoon yeast flakes, ½ hand basil, some pepper, some salt

Preparation
Cut the onion and fennel into small cubes. Put the fennel green aside for later.

Brown the onions and fennel together in the olive oil. Add the risotto rice until glassy. Deglaze with the white wine and reduce.

Add the pressed or finely chopped garlic.

Pour the vegetable stock into slowly and let it boil down while stirring, then let it boil down again and let it boil down again while stirring. The capers are added in about half the amount of vegetable broth.

At the end of the cooking time stir in the almond paste and the yeast flakes.

When the risotto is almost ready, add the whole lemon, the fennel green and the basil.

Now taste with pepper, lemon juice and a little salt. Ready!

Risotto (this or that) is a North Italian porridge dish made from rice, which is prepared in many variations.

Sunflowercream

Ingredients
250 g sunflower seeds, 500 ml water, 6 tablespoons soymilk, 1 tablespoon lemon juice, 1 teaspoon salt

Preparation
Soak sunflower seeds overnight in water.

Drain excess water.

Add soymilk, lemon juice and salt and puree finely.

Chili sin Carne

Ingredients
90 g soy granules, 100 g green seed - grist, ½ litres vegetable broth, 1 red pepper, 1 medium courgette, 1 large onion, 1 small tin of peeled tomatoes, 2 small tin of kidney beans, 1 small tin of peeled tomatoes, 1 small tin of grated beans, 1 small onions, 1 small onions, 1 small on. tin corn, 5 small red chilli peppers, 1 packet of strained tomatoes, 2 tbsp. fine sea salt, 1 tbsp. pepper, 1 pinch cayenne pepper, 1 pinch paprika powder, hot roses, 1 pinch sugar, 1 pinch tomato salt, 2 tbsp. dried basil, some tomato puree, if required chili powder, some oil for browning

Preparation
Soak the soy granules and green seed meal in the boiled vegetable stock and leave to swell for approx. 20 minutes.

Dice the onions and cut the peppers and courgettes into diagonal strips.

Finely chop the red chillies and chop the peeled tomatoes.

Heat the oil in a large pan or pot and fry the onions until translucent. Add the zucchini and peppers and sauté for about 5 minutes, then add the drained soy granules and green seed meal and fry for about 5-6 minutes while stirring.

Add the finely chopped tomatoes and the canned tomato juice, the tomatoes that have passed through and the chillies.

Then drain the kidney beans and corn and add to the pan.

Bring to the boil and season with the spices, herbs, sugar and tomato paste. Bring to the boil again and season to taste again.

Tip: Serve this dish with toasted bread.

Fun Fact
Chili sin Carne, short also only Chili mentioned, is the designation of a sharp court, which has its origin in the south of the United States. Mistakenly, it is always attributed to Mexican cuisine instead of Tex-Mex cuisine. This may also be connected with the redefinition of the southern border of the USA in the Treaty of Guadalupe Hidalgo in 1848 to the disadvantage of Mexico. As with many other dishes, in the case of Chili sin Carne there is also a dispute about the original origin, the right Ingredients and the spelling.

Chicken Fricassee

Ingredients
1 bag rice (possibly wild rice mixture), 50 g medium or fine soya - chopped, 100 g frozen or fresh peas, 1 glass asparagus, ½ shell fresh mushrooms, 250 ml vegetable broth, 250 ml soya milk, 1 tablespoon flour, 1 onion, some water, some oil, some salt and pepper, if required herbs of your choice, soya - cream or white wine

Preparation
First prepare the rice according to the instructions on the packet.

Peel and chop the onion. Clean the mushrooms. Drain the asparagus and cut into 1 cm long pieces.

Soak the soy slices in the broth according to the package instructions and then drain.

Fry the onions in a little oil until translucent. Add the broth. As soon as it boils, add the peas and the fresh mushrooms.

Simmer for about 10-15 minutes at medium heat until the vegetables are cooked. Now add the asparagus, the soymilk and the drained soy slices.

Mix the flour in a glass with a little water. Then slowly add to the boiling vegetables until the desired consistency is reached and simmer for another minute.

Season to taste with salt, pepper, herbs of your choice, soy cream and/or white wine.

Now arrange the fricassee with the side dishes and serve.

Lentil Bratlings

Ingredients
200 g lentils, 100 g onions, 100 g leek, 100 g carrots, 100 g mushrooms, 4 tbsp flour, 1 tsp curry, some salt and pepper, some herbs of your choice, olive oil for frying, chilli powder

Preparation
Soak the lenses overnight.

Chop onions, leeks, carrots, mushrooms and herbs coarsely and puree with the lentils (pour off the water), salt, pepper, curry, chilli. Then add the flour.

The mass is now quite sticky.

Now form with a tablespoon small bratlings and bake them in olive oil.

Paprika Mortadella

Ingredients
200 g flour, 4 tbsp yeast flakes/flakes, 2 tbsp instant vegetable stock, 1 tbsp garlic granules, 1 medium pepper, 1 small onion, 1 tbsp flour, 250 ml water, 30 ml neutral oil

Preparation
Wash and seed the peppers and peel the onions. Then dice both.

Add the flour to the diced Ingredients and stir in. The flour binds the liquid.

Now add the flour and stir well.

Now stir in the spices. Please keep to the order, otherwise the mortadella will be seasoned unevenly.

Make a small hollow in the mixture. Now pour the water and the oil into this trough and mix everything well. To make it easier to mix, you are also welcomed to add half the amount of water first.

Now roll the finished mortadella dough into baking paper and then into aluminium foil.

Steam the roll for only 1 hour. Then turn off the pot and let it cool.

Pizza with Yeast Melt

Ingredients
200 g spelt flour, 1/2 pck. fresh yeast, 100 ml lukewarm water, 2 tablespoons olive oil, 1 pinch sugar, 1 pinch salt, 4 tablespoons yeast flakes/flakes, 2 tablespoons vegan margarine, 3 teaspoons wheat flour, 150 ml lukewarm water, 1 teaspoon mustard, 100 ml tomato sauce, 1 half red pepper, 2 small onions, rosemary, oregano, garlic oil, some mild pickled peppers, some pitted olives

Preparation Pizza dough
Put 200 g flour in a bowl, please. Form a small hollow in which you crumble the yeast and add a pinch of sugar.

Mix with 100 ml lukewarm water, add some salt and 2 tbsp oil.

Depending on taste and desire, add the dried oregano.

Knead the dough well and then cover with a clean kitchen towel and leave to rise in a warm place for 30 minutes.

In the meantime, wash the paprika half, clean and cut into thin strips. Peel and halve the onions and cut them into thin rings. Remove the peppers from the glass, remove the stalk and cut into slices. Remove the olives from the glass and drain.

Knead the pizza dough well again, roll out thinly and spread with the tomato sauce. Cover with the vegetables.

Preparation of yeast melt
Melt the margarine in a small pot and stir in 3 teaspoons of flour with a whisk. Then add 150 ml water.

Add the yeast flakes, 1 teaspoon salt and some mustard. (Beware, the mustard should give taste, but not dominate). Bring to the boil while stirring, then drip over the pizza with a spoon.

Spread some oregano over the pizza to taste.

Bake in a preheated oven at 200 degrees until browned.

Tip: Depending on your taste, you can also topp the pizza with any other vegetable.

Cream Cheese

Ingredients
500 ml unsweetened soymilk, ½ lemon, 10 g coconut fat, 10 g sunflower oil, 1/2 tsp salt, 1 coffee filter

Preparation
Heat the soymilk. As soon as she starts cooking, turn the stove off.

Squeeze out half the lemon and pour the juice evenly into the soymilk. The soymilk is now flocculating.

Please keep stirring until no new flakes form. Then take the pot off the plate and let it cool for about 15 minutes.

Pour the mixture through a coffee filter and fill the contents of the filter into a bowl. There should be approx. 200 to 230 g in the filter. If necessary, stir in some of the drained liquid again if it has become too firm for your taste.

Stir in coconut fat and oil and season the cream cheese with salt.

Tip: The vegan cream cheese can be refined as desired with fresh or dried herbs and spices.

Meatballs with Vegetables

Ingredients
½ Tuber celery, ½ kohlrabi, 1 carrot, 1 red pepper, 50 g linseed, 1 tbsp mustard, 1 tbsp yeast flakes, 1 pinch salt, 1 pinch pepper

Preparation
Grate the vegetables, add the linseed, yeast flakes and mustard, season with pepper and salt and leave to stand for 2 hours.

Then form into small meatballs and, to make them firmer, squeeze out the vegetable juice a little.

Heat now some oil in a pan and fry the meatballs in it from both sides in approx. 15 minutes.

Meatballs

Ingredients
500 g tofu, 1 red onion, 1 white onion, 120 g breadcrumbs, 2 tbsp mustard, 1 bunch of smooth parsley, 8 cornichons, 1 tbsp soy flour, olive oil, for frying, salt and pepper, spices, as desired, instant vegetable stock

Preparation
First crush the tofu properly with your hands in a bowl.

Now put the onions, peeled and quartered, together with the cucumbers and parsley into the kitchen blender and chop into small pieces.

Now add the onion mix to the tofu. Now add the mustard, the breadcrumbs, the soy flour and all the spices. Take all the spices you like. Recommended: Chili powder, salt, black pepper from the mill, coriander, turmeric, soy sauce, oregano and possibly some vegetable broth.

Mix well with your hands until a nice dough is formed.

Form small balls with the help of a teaspoon and fry them brown all around for about 10 minutes.

Russian minced Meat Pot

Ingredients
150 g fine soy granules, 2 leeks, 2 large onions, 1 litre vegetable stock, 5 tbsp tomato puree, 1 tbsp medium hot mustard, 1 teaspoon salt, 1 teaspoon sugar, 1 teaspoon sweet paprika powder, 250 ml soy cream, possibly Harissa, pepper

Preparation
Prepare the soy slices according to the package instructions.

In the meantime, cut the leek into strips and dice the onions.

Fry the onions in oil and add the soy slices.

Add the leek with the tomato paste, broth, mustard and spices to the soy slices. Let simmer for about 15 minutes, stirring several times.

Finally stir in the soy whip. For a little more spiciness, add a little harissa.

Tortellini with smoked Tofu Spinach filling

Ingredients
Ingredients for the dough
200 g durum wheat semolina, 1 cup wheat flour, 1 cup cold water, some salt

Ingredients for the filling
175 g smoked tofu, 100 g deep-frozen spinach leaves, 1 clove garlic, some basil, fresh or deep-frozen, some salt, some water, breadcrumbs as required

Preparation
Preparation of the dough
Knead durum wheat semolina, flour, water and salt together by hand until a firm, preferably no longer sticky dough is obtained.

If the dough is too sticky, add a little more flour or water if it is too dry.

Wrap the finished dough in cling film and place in the refrigerator for about 30 minutes.

Preparation of the filling
Put the slightly chopped smoked tofu, the thawed spinach, the garlic clove and the spices in a high bowl and mix with a mixer.

Then add breadcrumbs to ensure a firm consistency as desired.

Take the dough out of the fridge and lay it out thinly on a floured work surface.

Cut out circles with a diameter of approx. 5 cm from the dough, e.g. with a drinking glass.

If the dough circles are not thin enough yet, increase them a little by hand.

Place a hazelnut-sized amount of the filling in the middle of each circle and moisten the edge with a little water.

Now the dough circle is formed into tortellini: First, fold the circle over the filling to form a semicircle and press the edges down well. The filling should now be completely enclosed.

The filled semi-circle is then brought into the shape of the moon, which works quite well, for example, by folding it around one's finger; in this step, the two ends are pressed together so that the tortellini remains in its typical shape.

The tortellini must not lie on top of each other before cooking, otherwise they may stick to each other.

Cook the tortellini in boiling salted water for about 5-8 minutes.

Tip: You can also prepare this dish with wholemeal flour.

Bulgur Curry

Ingredients
1 packet of coarse bulgur, 1 can of coconut milk, 4 potatoes, 1 can of chickpeas, 1 onion, curry powder, possibly curry paste, possibly garlic, possibly mushrooms

Preparation
Cook the bulgur as described on the packet.

Peel and boil the potatoes. When the bulgur and the potatoes are soft, drain both.

In a pan, sauté the onions and garlic a little. If you want to use mushrooms, fry them a little with it.

Then add the chickpeas, potatoes (sliced or diced), mix and then deglaze with the coconut milk.

Add plenty of curry powder and possibly curry paste until it takes on a pleasant yellow colour.

Now simmer for about 20 minutes.

Fun Fact
Bulgur is a pre-cooked (hydrothermally pre-treated) wheat. It is mainly made from durum wheat and is a staple food in Turkey and the Middle East. Bulgur, for example, can be cooked like rice with various vegetables. Similar to couscous in North Africa, it can also be eaten steamed or soaked without cooking, as taboulé or as Kısır (Bulgur salad). Bulgur is also an important ingredient for the court Çiğ Köfte, which is particularly widespread in the southeast of Turkey.

Spinach Noodle Dough

Ingredients
200 g wheat flour, type 1050, 200 g durum wheat semolina, 200 g deep-frozen spinach leaves, 3 tbsp olive oil, 1 tsp sea salt, 80 ml water

Preparation
Puree the defrosted and well dried spinach leaves very finely together with the salt.

Mix the flour with the durum wheat semolina. Press a hollow in the middle and add the spinach puree and the oil. Knead well with the water until a smooth dough is obtained.

Wrap the dough in cling film and place in the fridge for 1 hour.

The dough can be made into tagliatelle, ravioli, etc. as desired.

Chinese Cabbage Chopping Pan

Ingredients
125 g soy granules, 1 head of Chinese cabbage, cut into strips, 2 medium onions, 2 cloves of garlic, 200 ml soy cream or other vegetable cream substitute, boiling water, vegetable oil, salt and pepper as required, soy sauce

Preparation
Sprinkle the soy granules with salt, then sprinkle them with plenty of boiling water and let them steep for about 1/2 hour. It should be very soft then.

Then squeeze out well and fry in a large pan in hot oil. Season with salt, pepper and possibly soy sauce.

Peel the onion and garlic and chop both into small cubes.

Add the finely diced onions and simmer until glassy. Then add the diced garlic and simmer for about 1 - 2 minutes.

Add the Chinese cabbage cut into strips, put the lid on the pan and cook for about 5 - 10 minutes at medium heat. Finally add the cream, heat again and season to taste. Ready!

Country liver Sausage

Ingredients
200 g small brown lentils, ½ stick small chopped leek, 250 g sunflower seeds, 1 stem rosemary, 3 tbsp almond paste, 1 dash safflower oil, 1-2 tsp marjoram, dried, 1 lemon, grated rind thereof, 1 dash apple syrup, as required yeast flakes, some herbal salt, some pepper, some nutmeg

Preparation
Cook the lentils and leeks in water for about 25 minutes (the water should barely cover the lentils). Then allow to cool and puree.

Lightly roast the sunflower seeds without fat and grind very finely with the rosemary.

Stir the almond paste with a little water until smooth, stir the remaining Ingredients into the almond paste, mix well and add yeast flakes as required.

Spaghettini with Cherry Tomatoes and Balsamic Vinegar

Ingredients
400 g thin spaghetti, (spaghettini), 8 tablespoons olive oil, 2 dried small chilli peppers, 15 leaves basil, 2 tablespoons balsamic vinegar, 25 cherry tomatoes, sugar, herbs of Provence, some salt and pepper, Parmesan, as much as you like

Preparation
Heat the olive oil in a pan. Cut the cherry tomatoes in half and sauté in olive oil, season with salt and pepper. Crumble the chilli over it and add 1 good pinch of sugar. Add the balsamic vinegar and Provence herbs.

Cover the pan and simmer over a low heat. As soon as the tomatoes are soft, crush them lightly with a fork.

Cook the spaghettini according to the instructions on the packet until al dente and drain. Immediately mix with the braised tomatoes, cut the basil into fine strips and sprinkle over them.

Fun Fact
Aceto Balsamico or balsamic vinegar is a vinegar from the Italian province of Modena or the region of Emilia-Romagna. It has a dark brown colour and a sweet and sour taste. It is produced without balsa plants; the name refers to the fragrant character (balm means "fragrance") of this vinegar. In the case of balsamic vinegar, a distinction must be made between the traditional 'Aceto Balsamico Tradizionale di Modena' and the mass product 'Aceto Balsamico di Modena'.

Raw Vegetable Lasagna

Ingredients
2 small celeriac tubers, 2 beetroot, 2 tbsp cider vinegar, 2 medium carrots, 18 dried tomatoes, 2 tbsp hazelnuts, 4 tbsp olive oil, 2 handfuls pine nuts, 1.5 tsp freshly ground black pepper, 4 handfuls basil, 2 handfuls sunflower seeds, 2 handfuls pumpkin seeds, 2 Msp chili powder, 1.5 tsp salt, 2 small cloves garlic, water

Preparation
Cut the beetroot into fine slices and pour apple vinegar over it and leave to stand.

For the red pesto, finely chop the dried tomatoes.

Add the pine nuts, 1 tablespoon olive oil, chilli powder and some water to the dried tomatoes and puree with a hand blender.

For the green pesto, finely chop the basil leaves, hazelnuts and garlic clove. Add the sunflower and pumpkin seeds, 1 tablespoon olive oil, salt and black pepper and a little water. Make the green pesto more liquid by adding more water than the red pesto.

Cut the carrots and celery into very fine slices.

Now pour some of the green pesto onto the plates and spread over the surface. Then layer the vegetables and alternately distribute the red and green pesto between the vegetable layers.

If you want to make the raw vegetable lasagne as a starter, then the indicated quantity is sufficient for 4-6 people.

Fun Fact

According to a less widespread theory, there should be an English origin for the court: In the 14th century Forme of Cury, a collection of recipes prepared by chefs at the court of King Richard II of England, the dish "loseyns" (pronounced "lasan") is described, which also contains layered pasta plates baked with cheese.

Spaghetti with Sugar Peas and Cherry Tomatoes

Ingredients
400 g spaghetti, 260 g snow peas, 20 small cherry tomatoes, 2 cloves of garlic, 4 large fresh chilli peppers, 4 spring onions

Olive oil for frying

Preparation
Thread off the sugar snap peas if necessary.

Cut leek onions into thin rings, peel garlic and chop into small pieces, halve chilli peppers, pit and cut crosswise into very thin strips, halve cherry tomatoes.

Now boil the pasta in salted water al dente.

Meanwhile, fry the sugar snap peas lightly in plenty of olive oil, then add the remaining Ingredients and just heat well.

Add the cooked spaghetti and serve.

Stuffed Peppers with green Spelt

Ingredients
3 peppers, 150 g green seed, 320 ml vegetable stock, 3 medium onions, 3 tbsp tomato paste, salt and pepper, 200 ml strained tomatoes, basil, paprika powder. harissa

Preparation
Preheat the oven to 170 degrees.

The peppers "cut off" and hollow out. Please pick up the lid.

Cut the green stem out of the lid so that the lid becomes a wreath.

Put the green kernel in a pot, pour hot vegetable broth over it and let it swell for 5 minutes over a low heat and stirring constantly.

Season the green seeds with tomato paste and spices. Finally fold in the onion rings. Take off the stove.

Season the tomatoes to taste with basil, salt and pepper and pour into an ovenproof dish.

Fill the peppers with the green seed mixture, place the wreath lid on top and add to the tomato sauce.

Put everything in the oven and bake for about 20 - 25 minutes.

If the paprika wreath turns too brown, simply cover it with aluminium foil.

Fun Fact
Green spelt (also called "Badischer Reis") is the grain of spelt that is harvested half ripe and artificially dried immediately afterwards. Originally the spelt was harvested as a reaction to bad weather periods, which

destroyed the harvest, before ripening (in the so-called "dough ripeness" with approx. 50 % grain moisture). Since the dried kernels - boiled with water - were tasty, the tradition of harvesting part of the spelt as green grain developed.

Apple red Cabbage

Ingredients
1 red cabbage, 1 apple, 1 teaspoon salt, 1 teaspoon sugar, 1 pinch pepper

Preparation
Cut the red cabbage into small pieces and cook for 20 minutes with the sugar, salt and pepper.

Cut the apple into pieces and after 10 minutes add to the red cabbage.

Drain excess water after cooking time. Ready!

Eggplant Ragout

Ingredients
1 small eggplant (approx. 300g), 1 small onion, 3 spring onions, 1-2 cloves of garlic, ½ chilli pepper, 1 tablespoon tomato puree, ½ cup of vegetable stock, 500g tomato passata, 1 tablespoon vinegar, ½ TL dried basil, ½ TL dried marjoram, 1 tablespoon paprika powder, 1 pr cayenne pepper, 1 pinch pepper and salt, 6 leaves fresh basil, olive oil

Preparation
Dice the eggplant. Peel and eighth the onion. Cut the chilli pepper into thin rings.

Fry the aubergine, onion and chilli in plenty of olive oil. Add the tomato paste and fry. Then deglaze with vinegar.

Add the vegetable stock.

Peel the garlic and cut into thin slices. Add.

Add the tomato passata, spices and dried herbs.

Remove roots and dark green ends of spring onions, cut white and light green parts into rings, add.

Simmer at low heat for 10-15 minutes.

Season to taste with salt and olive oil.

Tip: Serve with noodles, rice, millet, quinoa or similar. Cut the basil leaves into strips and sprinkle over them.

Eggplant Spaghetti

Ingredients
250g spaghetti, 1 small eggplant (about 200 g), 1 onion, 1 tablespoon margarine, 1 tablespoon yeast flakes, ½ T soymilk, pepper and salt

Preparation
Peel the onion and cut into rings.

Melt the margarine with a little salt and sauté the onion.

Cut the aubergine lengthwise into thin slices and the slices lengthwise into very thin strips (about 2 mm thick).

Add to the onions and fry.

Cook the spaghetti in plenty of salted water until al dente and then drain.

When the aubergines are cooked, stir in the yeast flakes.

Add the soymilk and boil down a little.

Mix with the spaghetti.

Tip: The indicated amount of spaghetti is as much as in a ring of thumb and index finger.

Cauliflower on Noodles

Ingredients
1 cauliflower (about 500 g), 2 tbsp margarine, 1 tbsp flour, 1/2 tb soymilk, 3 tbsp lemon juice, 1 tbsp cinnamon juice, 1 tbsp margarine EL potato or corn starch, 2 EL yeast flakes, 250g ribbon noodles, Farfalle or similar. 1 tablespoon vermicelli (vermicelli) or broken ribbon noodles, some salt

Preparation
Divide the cauliflower into small florets and cut the stems crosswise. Covered with lightly salted water do not soften for 10-12 minutes (stalk also boil along).

Melt 1 tablespoon margarine in a pan, stir in flour until it has combined with the margarine. Slowly add the vegetable boiling water and stir until smooth. Reduce by half.

Cook the ribbon noodles or farfalle in salted water until al dente.

Roast vermicelli or broken noodles uncooked in 1/2 tablespoon margarine.

Mix the starch with the milk and add to the sauce with lemon juice and 1 teaspoon salt.

Bring to the boil again, stir in yeast flakes and 1/2 tablespoon margarine.

Arrange the cauliflower florets on a bed of noodles, add the sauce and roasted noodles.

Tip: Use 1-2 tsp mustard instead of lemon juice. Boiled potatoes instead of noodles.

Curry Noodle Pan

Ingredients
250g spaghetti, 1 tsp turmeric, 1 onion, 3 small courgettes, 250-300g mushrooms, 1 tsp ground cumin, 1 tablespoon curry powder, 4 tablespoons chives or parsley (fresh or frozen), 2 tablespoons soy sauce, sesame oil for frying, pepper and salt

Preparation
Break the spaghetti into four parts (quarter them), boil and add the turmeric to the boiling water.

Cut the mushrooms and courgettes into thin slices.

Cut the onion into half slices and fry with 1 tablespoon of oil for 2 minutes at the highest heat.

Add the mushrooms and fry for 3 minutes.

Add zucchini, cumin, curry powder and fry for 3-5 minutes.

Add spaghetti, soy sauce, pepper, chives/parsley and mix well.

Tip: Tastes good with 1/2 Hokkaido pumpkin instead of zucchini.

Steam Noodles

Ingredients
2 T flour, 2 T lukewarm soymilk, 1 tablespoon sugar, 1/2 cube yeast, 1 tablespoon margarine, 1 vegan vanilla sauce

Preparation
For the yeast dumplings, place the flour in a bowl and form a hollow in the middle.

Pour 1/2 t soymilk halfway into the trough, add the sugar and the crumbled yeast.

Slowly knead with the surrounding flour, adding just under 1/2 t soymilk until a firm yeast dough is obtained.

Form 4 balls from the dough, place them on a floured base and leave to rise for approx. 20 minutes in a warm, draught-free place.

Then put the remaining soymilk and margarine in a large pan with a lid and heat.

When the soymilk is so warm that the margarine has dissolved, put the yeast dumplings in it and close with the lid.

Bring the milk to the boil and then simmer at medium heat for another 10 minutes.

Place the steamed noodles on two plates and add the vanilla sauce.

Tip: As a main course for two, as a dessert for four. Fresh fruit or compote also goes well with this.

Potato Goulash

Ingredients
4 potatoes, 2 onions, 1 red pepper, 1 yellow pepper, 2 cloves of garlic, 2 tbsp vegetable stock, 2 tbsp tomato paste, 1 tbsp vinegar, 1 tbsp margarine (optional), paprika powder, pepper, parsley, celery herb (optional), oil

Preparation
Peel potatoes and onions and cut into bite-sized pieces.

Clean the peppers and cut into bite-sized pieces.

All together now sauté in oil.

Add tomato paste, fry.

Deglaze with vinegar and vegetable stock.

Add the remaining Ingredients (but: herbs only shortly before the end of the cooking time), cook at medium heat for about 20 minutes until the potatoes are done.

Potato Dumplings

Ingredients
1 t cold mashed potatoes, 1 t flour, salt

Preparation
Knead the mashed potatoes, flour and salt together, divide into four parts and form dumplings.

Pour into plenty of boiling salted water, then put the heat down immediately and let it draw on low heat until the dumplings float to the surface.

Remove with a skimmer.

Tip: You can also fill the dumplings with fried onions or white bread croutons before cooking.

Chickpeas and Beans Stew

Ingredients
250 g chickpeas, 1 t white quail beans (or kidney beans), 2 onions, 1 bell pepper, 1-2 tomatoes, 1 tbsp tomato paste, 3 garlic cloves, 2 tbsp soy sauce, ½ T vegetable broth, 1 pr sugar, oil, salt, herb salt, pepper, paprika powder

Preparation
Soak chickpeas and beans overnight.

Cook the chickpeas for almost an hour, the beans for about an hour.

Peel and chop the onion.

Cut the peppers into rhombuses.

Dice the tomatoes.

Fry the onions in a little oil until translucent.

Add the paprika and fry.

Fry the tomato paste on the bottom of the pot with the sugar.

Add the beans and chickpeas and deglaze with the vegetable stock.

Peel and finely chop the garlic and add to the tomatoes.

Flavour with soy sauce, salt and the spices.

Pumpkin Ragout

Ingredients
½ Hokkaido pumpkin, 1 t soymilk, 2 tbsp margarine, 2 tbsp flour, 1 tbsp yeast flakes, 1 pr nutmeg, salt

Preparation
Remove the seeds and fibres from the pumpkin and cut into pieces about 2x2 centimetres in size.

Melt the margarine in a pot and sauté the pumpkin in it.

Stir in the flour until it has combined with the margarine.

Slowly add the soymilk. Stir diligently so that no clumps will form.

Add yeast flakes and season with salt and nutmeg.

Cook on a low heat for 10-15 minutes until the pumpkin cubes are soft. Stir it from time to time. Ready!

Schnetzel pan

Ingredients
100 g coarse soya slices, 1 glass of corn, 1 glass of kidney beans, 1 large onion, chopped small, 2-4 cloves of garlic, chopped small, oil, herb salt, pepper, curry, paprika, turmeric, soya sauce, herb mustard, yeast broth, yeast flakes

Preparation
Soak the soy slices with water and soy sauce according to instructions on the packet.

Brown the onion and garlic in oil. Add the Schnetzel to the pan with the soaking water.

Season to taste with the spices, mustard and yeast broth, then add the corn and beans. Add some soy sauce if necessary.

Finally sprinkle with yeast flakes and stir well again.

Serve with rice or noodles.

Vegetable Paella

Ingredients
1 cup Basmati rice, 2 cups water, 5 runner beans, 1 carrot, 1 onion, 100 g mushrooms, 250 g peas from the jar, 1 leek, 1-2 tomatoes, oil

Preparation
Boil the rice in water and then let it swell to a very low level.

Cut the vegetables into small pieces and sauté in oil.

Season to taste with spices of your choice.

Finally mix in the rice.

Spaghetti with Garlic, Oil and Pepper

Ingredients
400 g spaghetti, 4 garlic cloves, 1 dried pepper, 5 tablespoons olive oil, 2 tablespoons parsley, salt

Preparation
Cook the spaghetti until al dente.

Chop the garlic and parsley.

Brown the garlic and the grated pepper in oil until yellowish, salt and sprinkle with the parsley.

Mix with the cooked spaghetti and serve immediately.

Hokkaido Pumpkin Lasagna

Ingredients
1 Hokkaido pumpkin, 1 onion, 6-8 leaves fresh green cabbage, 200 g fresh herbs, 150 g vegan cheese (e.g. Santeciano from Vegourmet), lasagne leaves, vegan vegetable stock, olive oil, soymilk, vegan margarine or Alsan, flour, fresh nutmeg, salt and pepper

Preparation
Cut the pumpkin into pieces, remove the seeds and cut into small 1-2 cm large pieces.

Clean the herb mushrooms and cut them into slices.

Remove the thick stalk from the kale and cut it into strips.

Chop the onion into small pieces and sauté in a pan with olive oil until translucent.

Add the kale strips and fry for a few minutes. Then move aside.

Heat some olive oil in a large saucepan, add the pumpkin pieces and the herbs. Deglaze with approx. 200 ml vegetable stock and simmer for approx. 5 minutes.

Now grate the vegan cheese.

Preheat the oven to approx. 180°C.

For the béchamel sauce, heat approx. 250 ml soymilk with 4-5 tbsp margarine and 4-5 tbsp flour while stirring constantly. Depending on the desired consistency, add a little more flour or soymilk.

Season the sauce with salt and pepper and freshly grated nutmeg.

Now line a greased casserole dish with the first layer of lasagne sheets. Then layer the kale, pumpkin mushrooms, sauce and cheese in order until the **Ingredients** are used up or the baking dish is filled. Finish with lasagne leaves and then add béchamel sauce and vegan cheese.

Place the lasagne in the oven for about 20-30 minutes.

Fun Fact
Hokkaido pumpkin is the name given to several small varieties of the giant pumpkin originating from the Japanese island Hokkaidō

They are broad-round, orange-red pumpkins weighing between 1 and 2 kilograms, the thin skin of which - unlike most other pumpkin varieties - softens when cooked and can be eaten with the pumpkin - the seeds and fibres should be removed. The flesh has a nutty aroma similar to chestnut and a stable consistency, although it contains hardly any noticeable fibres. This pumpkin variety adapts to many flavours, but harmonises particularly well with ginger and chilli and can be used for soups, casseroles or as a vegetable. The Hokkaido pumpkin can also be eaten raw or used in salads.

The seeds of Hokkaido are dried. They can then be sown or eaten. The thickness of the core shell can vary, so they are not always tasty.

Chili Spinach Risotto with Lemon Grass

Ingredients
300-400 g fresh baby spinach, 1-2 red chilli peppers, 1 organic lemon, 2 lemon grass stems, 300 g risotto rice, 1 large shallot, 2 cloves of garlic, 1200 ml vegan vegetable stock, 300 ml vegan non-alcoholic white wine, 70g freshly grated vegan cheese, some salt and pepper, olive oil, chili threads

Preparation
Wash the baby spinach and cut it into fine strips. Finely dice the shallots and garlic.

Grate the lemon zest and then squeeze out the lemon. Now remove the seeds from the chillies and cut them into small pieces. Wash and clean the lemongrass and make a knot out of each stick.

Now sauté the shallots and the garlic in olive oil. Add the rice and stir well. After 1 minute, add the white wine and simmer.

Now add the lemongrass knots, then gradually add the vegetable stock and cook the risotto for about 20 minutes stirring constantly.

About 5 minutes before the end of cooking, remove the lemon grass and add the grated lemon zest and spinach leaves.

Stir well and season to taste with lemon juice, salt, pepper and chilli threads. Before serving, stir in the grated cheese and season to taste again. Bon appetit!

Fun Fact
Risotto is a North Italian rice porridge that can be prepared in many variations.

Pasta Bavette with fresh Mint and Peasauce

Ingredients
500 g Pasta Bavette, 1 bunch fresh mint, 300 g frozen peas, 1 large fennel tuber, 1 onion, 100 g vegan cheese, 1 lemon, 150 ml white wine, 1 packet soy cream, some salt and pepper, olive oil

Preparation
Wash the fennel bulb and plane it into fine strips.

Separate the mint leaves from the stalks and chop coarsely.

Finely chop the onion, grate the cheese, squeeze the lemon.

Sauté the onion in olive oil and add about half of the frozen peas. Cook the remaining peas briefly in boiling water.

Now deglaze everything with white wine and simmer for a few minutes.

Add the soy whip and puree finely. Depending on the consistency, add a little water, cream or white wine.

Cook the pasta according to the instructions on the packet, then mix with the pea sauce, the fennel slices, the cheese and the mint leaves.

Season with lemon juice, a little salt and pepper.

Sprinkle the peas, which you have cooked separately, over it and garnish everything with a little green.

Mushroom Burger

Ingredients
500 g mushrooms, 1 to 2 onions, 2 tablespoons sunflower oil, 2 cloves of garlic, 2 slices dry white bread, 1 teaspoon medium hot mustard, 60 g cashew nuts, 1 tablespoon chopped parsley, 1 egg replacer (available in the health food store), 2 tablespoons breadcrumbs, 4 hamburger rolls, salad leaves, hamburger sauce, some salt, black pepper from the mill

Preparation
Clean the mushrooms and chop them into coarse pieces.

Now peel the onion and dice it into fine pieces.

Peel the garlic and press it through with a garlic press.

Now heat the sunflower oil in a pan and add the onion cubes and the pressed garlic. These let them fry in it. But please make sure that you don't tan either of them too much!

Add the mushrooms and fry briefly over high heat while turning.

Now pour the Ingredients from the pan into a bowl and let it cool down a little.

Next, crumble the white bread slices well.

Put four of the cashew nuts aside, chop the rest finely.

Add the breadcrumbs with mustard, egg substitute, the cashew nuts, salt, pepper and 1 tablespoon breadcrumbs to the mushroom mixture in the bowl and mix the Ingredients well.

Heat some oil in a pan again and form four burgers with wet hands. If the mixture is too moist for your needs, simply add some breadcrumbs.

Fry in hot fat on both sides until golden brown.

Cut the rolls open and cover each with salad leaves and burgers, cheese and hamburger sauce, garnish with cashew nut and serve. Ketchup and hamburger cheese can also be added if desired.

Tofu Schnitzel

Ingredients
400g tofu, 50g ground almonds, ½ lemon, 4 tbsp oil, some salt and pepper, some nutmeg

Preparation
Cut the tofu into slices and squeeze out the lemon. Put the lemon juice in a deep plate.

For the breading, mix some salt, pepper, nutmeg and the almonds in a second-deep plate.

Now the tofu slices are first soaked in the lemon juice and then rolled in the almond mixture.

Fry the escalopes in oil until crispy. It's done!

Bratwurst

Ingredients
300 g seitan flour, 30 g yeast flakes, 1 clove garlic, 2 Msp. cumin, 4 tsp. paprika powder, 2 Msp. pepper, 3 tsp. salt, 2 pinches sugar, 2 tsp. onion powder, 6 tbsp. oil, 1 tsp. mustard, 4 tbsp. soy sauce, 6 tbsp. tomato puree, 350 ml water

Preparation
Place in a bowl Seitan flour, cumin, garlic, yeast flakes, paprika, salt, pepper and onion powder.

In a second bowl add the oil, mustard, soy sauce, tomato paste and water.

Mix the Ingredients well in each bowl, the liquid Ingredients best with a whisk.

Pour the liquid Ingredients into the dry Ingredients and knead well.

Now form 10-12 sausages with a diameter of approx. 2 cm.

Wrap the sausages first in baking paper and then firmly in aluminium foil.

Bake in the oven at 180°C for 50 minutes, then turn off the oven and let the sausages rest in the oven for another 15 minutes. Remove from oven and unwrap immediately.

Tip: You can also freeze the sausages. The sausages taste cold and warm, can be fried or cut into soups. If you're planning a barbecue, get on the grill. Surely you can also vary the spices.

Beanburger

Ingredients
250g kidney beans, 4 tbsp oat flakes, 1 large carrot, 1 large onion, 1 garlic clove, 2 tbsp olive oil, black pepper, ground coriander, parsley, thyme, salt, optional: flour or gluten powder

To cover the burgers
4 burger rolls, rocket, 2 avocados, 1-2 tomatoes, mango-balsamic mustard

Preparation
Peel the onion, cut into small cubes and fry in a pan with hot oil until glassy.

Put the kidney beans with the pressed garlic viscosity, the previously fried onion, the carrot (grated) and the remaining Ingredients for the burgers in a bowl.

Crush the mass or purée it a little. It is not bad if the bean mixture has not become completely fine and can still contain a few pieces after mashing. Who would like a somewhat firmer mass can still add some gluten powder or flour.

Heat some oil in a pan and add 1/4 of the mixture with a ladle and flatten a little.

First fry the burgers from one side, then turn them over and fry them from the other side.

Spread one half of each roll with mango-balsamic mustard and cover with avocados, rocket and tomato slices.

Another Burger, just different.

Ingredients
250 g smoked tofu, 50 g peanuts, 4 burgers rolls, 2 bananas, 2 tbsp soy sauce, 2 tbsp sesame paste, 1 onion, 1 garlic cloves, 50 g flour, 1 beef tomato, ½ cucumber, 1 tbsp mustard, peanut butter, sugar, salt and pepper, iceberg lettuce as required

Preparation
Chop half a banana, onion, peanuts and garlic into small pieces. In a bowl mix with the flour, mustard, soy sauce and sesame paste.

Add the smoked tofu, season with salt and pepper and knead well until the mixture is nice. Form 4 burger roasts and dust them on both sides with a little flour.

Heat the oil in a large pan and fry the burgers on both sides until crispy. But be careful when turning, because the burgers are not quite as stable in the beginning.

At the same time caramelise the sugar in a second pan as desired.

Meanwhile, cut the remaining 1 ½ bananas into thin slices and add them to the caramelized sugar. Turn off the stove and take out the bananas.

Now roast the burger rolls in the oven or on the toaster. Spread the peanut butter on top as desired, cover with iceberg lettuce, tomato and cucumber slices as desired and place the burgers on top.

Finally, the caramelized bananas and the lid on top.

Seitanschnitzel Gypsy style

Ingredients
2 seitan schnitzel, 6 tbsp soy cream, 2 tbsp Ajvar, 1 onion, 150 ml vegetable stock, 1 pepper, 1 glass puszta salad, 1 egg substitute, 100 ml white wine, salt and pepper, paprika powder, tabasco, chili powder, tomatoes, breadcrumbs

Preparation
Wash the pepper, remove seeds and cut into thin strips.

Drain the glass with the pusztasalad.

Bread the seitan schnitzel, season and fry on both sides. Then keep warm.

Fry the onions in a pan until translucent, then add the paprika and puszta salad and stir in the soy cream.

Add the broth, strained tomatoes, Ajvar and the white wine. Let simmer until the vegetables have the desired bite.

Finally season and place the seitan schnitzel in the sauce and leave to simmer for a short time.

Cauliflower Schnitzel

Ingredients
1 cauliflower, 2 tbsp flour, 2 eggs, 50 g breadcrumbs, 100 g butter, ground pepper, salt

Preparation
Wash the whole cauliflower and boil it whole in salted water. Make sure that the cauliflower does not become too soft.

Cut the drained and cooled cauliflower into slices.

Mix the flour with some salt and pepper in a deep plate. Whisk the eggs in a second-deep plate and put the breadcrumbs in a third deep plate. Now turn each cauliflower slice first in the flour, then in the egg and finally in the breadcrumbs.

Fry the cauliflower escalopes on both sides in the hot butter.

Meatballs

Ingredients
100 g soy granules, 2 onions, 2 tablespoons parsley, 1 teaspoon medium hot mustard, 7 tablespoons breadcrumbs, 3 tablespoons heaped soy flour, salt and pepper, 2 tablespoons sweet paprika powder, 2 cloves garlic, 2 tablespoons soy sauce, oil for frying

Preparation
Put all Ingredients in a bowl and knead well.

Season to taste with salt and spices as required.

Form medium sized meatballs and fry in a pan in some oil until golden brown.

Tofu - Meatballs

Ingredients
50 g firm natural tofu, 1 small onion, 1 tbsp soy flour, 2 tbsp water, salt and pepper as required, soy sauce as required, mustard if desired, breadcrumbs if desired, a little oil if desired

Preparation
Drain the tofu and crumble in a bowl with a fork or your hands.

Peel the onion and cut into small cubes.

Mix the soy flour with the water in a separate bowl and then add to the tofu together with the onions.

Season to taste with salt, pepper, soy sauce and mustard and knead well.

Now form meatballs from the mixture. If the mixture does not hold together, add some breadcrumbs and knead again. If necessary, it may help to add a little more of the soy flour-water mixture.

Fry the meatballs in the oil which has not been heated too much. They should be brown on both sides.

Tip: The meatballs go very well with vegetables and mashed potatoes.

French Fries from the Oven

Ingredients
1 kg potatoes, 2 teaspoons sweet paprika powder, ½ teaspoon salt, ½ teaspoon mixed and dried, herbs, 3 tablespoons neutral oil, garlic powder

Preparation
Peel the potatoes and cut them into chopsticks. Cut the peeled potatoes into slices and then put them on top of each other and cut them into sticks. Place the potato sticks briefly in water.

Before preparing, drain well and dab dry with kitchen paper.

Place the potato sticks in a bowl and mix well with the paprika powder, garlic powder, salt, herbs and oil with your hands. Then place on a baking tray lined with baking paper.

Bake in a preheated oven at 200°C for approx. 35 minutes. Then turn the oven up to 220°C and let the chips brown for another 10 minutes. Season to taste with salt and serve.

Fun Fact
The oldest known reference to the Preparation of French fries dates back to 1781 by Joseph Gérard:

"The inhabitants of Namur, Huy and Dinant have the habit of fishing in the Meuse, then frying this catch to expand their menu (especially poor people). When the waters are frozen and fishing is difficult, the inhabitants cut potatoes into fish form and fry them. This procedure is more than a hundred years old.

Curry - Vegetables with Tofu

Ingredients
60 g sultanas, 2 tbsp oil, 1 onion, 1 clove garlic, 1 tbsp fresh ginger, 2 tsp curry, 1 tsp cumin, 1 tsp ground coriander, 1 tsp turmeric, 1 tsp salt, 250 g carrots, 2 red chilli peppers, 250 g broccoli, 250 g cauliflower, 250 g solid tofu, 1 can coconut milk, 1 lime, 1 tbsp brown sugar, 60 cashews, soy sauce

Preparation
Soak the sultanas in lukewarm water for about 20 minutes.

Cut the tofu into cubes and sprinkle with soy sauce. Cover and leave to stand for approx. 10 minutes.

Fry the tofu cubes crispy in a pan with 1 tablespoon of oil, deglaze with soy sauce and put aside on a plate.

Heat the oil again in a pan, add the onion, garlic and ginger and steam for 5 minutes over medium heat.

Sprinkle with spices and salt. Steam for 5 minutes while stirring. Pour the mixture into a saucepan.

Drain the soaked sultanas, drain and add to the pot with the carrots, peppers, broccoli, cauliflower and tofu.

Add coconut milk and cook for 15-20 minutes at low heat until the vegetables are almost soft.

Season curry vegetables with lime juice and brown sugar. Sprinkle with cashew nuts and serve immediately.

Indian Lentil Stew

Ingredients
2 tbsp oil, 2 tsp curry, 1 bunch spring onions, 400 ml vegetable stock, 1 piece fresh ginger, walnut-sized, 2 cloves garlic, 200 ml coconut milk, 250 g red lentils, 2 peppers, 2 pinches pepper, 1 tsp salt, 1 tsp mustard seed, 1 small glass peeled tomatoes

Preparation
Chop the garlic and ginger into small pieces, cut the spring onions into rings and the paprika into cubes.

Roast the curry powder and the mustard seeds in a hot pot.

Then add oil, garlic and ginger. Fry briefly and then add the lentils and the paprika cubes and fry briefly.

Deglaze with the vegetable stock and bring to the boil.

Add the peeled tomatoes and the coconut milk and simmer at low heat for approx. 15 - 20 minutes until the lentils are soft.

Finally mix in the spring onions and season with salt and pepper.

Hack - Noodle - Casserole

Ingredients
1 zucchini, 1 carrot, 1 onion, 2 cloves of garlic, ½ tube of tomato paste, 1 sachet of strained tomatoes, 1 pinch of sugar, 1 sachet of sugar. soy cream, 300 g soy granules, 3 tbsp gyros spice mixture, 3 tbsp neutral oil, 500 g noodles, 300 ml soy milk, 4 tbsp margarine, 3 ½ tbsp yeast flakes, 1 tbsp salt, ½ tbsp medium hot mustard, 3 handfuls flour, if required water, some salt and pepper, oil, thyme

Preparation
Soak the soy granules in hot water and then squeeze them out well.

Mix a marinade from the oil, gyros spice and neutral oil, stir into the soy granules and leave to stand overnight in the refrigerator.

Cook the pasta according to the instructions on the packet and drain.

Wash and dice the carrot, onions and courgettes and fry them in a large pan or wok with oil and garlic and the soy granules and the rest of the marinade. During this time, you should be patient, as the marinade has to cook a little first.

Then add the tomato paste and the tomatoes. If necessary, add a little water and simmer a little.

Add a pinch of sugar, salt, pepper and thyme to the sauce, stir in the soy whip after about 3-4 minutes and turn off the heat. Add the cooked pasta to the sauce and stir well.

Grease a casserole dish and add the pasta mixture.

To melt the yeast, boil the soymilk, margarine, mustard, salt, pepper and yeast flakes and bind them with the flour. It should be a creamy mass.

Then pour this mixture over the casserole and bake at 200-220°C until the yeast melt is brown.

Pasta Dough

Ingredients
400 g durum wheat semolina, 180 ml warm water, salt to boil

Preparation
Collect the durum wheat semolina on a work surface and press a hollow into the middle.

Then gradually add a total of 180 ml of very warm water, so that the semolina quickly becomes elastic when kneaded. Then push the semolina into the water trough from the outside, so that a thick mass is formed.

Now knead the semolina and water with your hands until you have a nice, elastic and smooth dough.

Due to the warm water the semolina quickly loses its crumb shape and after 10 minutes the dough is smooth and homogeneous. It must no longer stick, even the hands should be dry and without adhering dough residue, then enough has been kneaded.

Now the dough is wrapped in cling film and should rest for at least 30 minutes.

After 30 minutes of waiting, form the noodles. You determine the form.

Cook the pasta in salted water for about 3-4 minutes. The water should no longer boil bubbly.

As soon as the noodles float upstairs, they're done.

Spaghetti Napoli

Ingredients
500 g spaghetti, 1 onion, 1 tablespoon olive oil, 500 g tomatoes, 1 teaspoon vegetable stock, 1 teaspoon dried oregano, 1 teaspoon dried basil, 1 teaspoon rosemary, paprika powder, salt and pepper, sugar

Preparation
Cook the spaghetti in plenty of salted water until al dente.

Peel the onion and chop finely.

Heat the oil in a saucepan and fry the onion while stirring.

Add the strained tomatoes, dissolve the vegetable stock in it and cook for 10 minutes on a low heat.

Add the herbs and let everything cook for another 5 minutes.

Season the sauce with paprika, pepper and sugar and serve with the well-drained spaghetti.

Onion Tart

Ingredients

150 g flour (type 405), 100 g spelt flour, 1 cube yeast, 1 tsp sugar, 150 ml water, 1/2 tsp salt, 4 tbsp olive oil, 500 g onions, 200 g mushrooms, 1 bunch flat parsley, 2 tbsp caraway seeds, 200 g tofu, some salt and pepper

Preparation

Dissolve the yeast and sugar in some of the warm water and mix with flour to a dough. Leave this dough to rise for 15 minutes.

Add the spelt flour, salt, oil and plenty of warm water until the dough separates from the bowl.

Allow to rise for about 30 to 45 minutes until the dough has doubled in volume.

Peel onions, cut into very thin rings.

clean mushrooms, cut into thin slices

Now fry the onions until translucent and then add the mushrooms and fry briefly.

Puree the tofu and parsley (possibly add some water to obtain a spreadable mass).

Season to taste with salt and pepper.

Roll out the dough on a baking tray and spread with the tofu mixture.

Spread the onions and mushrooms on top. Sprinkle with caraway seeds.

Bake in a preheated oven at 220°C for about 30 minutes until the surface is browned.

Pizza Garlic Champignon Paprika

Ingredients
For the dough:
300 g wheat flour (type 550), 1 sachet dry yeast, 1 teaspoon salt, 170 ml water

For the topping:
6 tbsp garlic oil or olive oil, 1 tbsp tomato puree, 2 red peppers or vegetable peppers, 250 g mushrooms, 1 onion, some salt and pepper, fresh or dried Italian herbs, harissa, garlic as required

Preparation
Place the Ingredients for the dough in a bowl, knead and leave to rise for about 40 minutes in a warm place.

In the meantime, peel any number of garlic cloves and dice finely.

Peel and dice the onion, clean and chop the peppers and mushrooms.

Mix the oil with the tomato paste, salt and pepper.

Roll out the finished dough and place on a baking tray. Spread the oil mixture evenly over the dough with a baking brush, then cover with the garlic, mushrooms, paprika and onions.

Now season the pizza with salt, pepper, herbs and harissa and bake at 250°C for about 10 - 15 minutes.

The dough can of course be topped with all kinds of vegetables and other Ingredients.

Dips and Sauces

Mayonnaise

Ingredients
3 tablespoons lemon juice, 75 ml soy drink, ¼ TL mustard, 1 pinch salt, 1 pinch paprika powder, 6 tablespoons oil

Preparation
Put all Ingredients, except the oil, in a blender. Switch on the lowest level.

Add the oil drop by drop until the mixture thickens. Continue mixing until the mixture is thick and smooth.

Store in a screw glass in the refrigerator.

Hummus

Ingredients
250 g dried chickpeas, 2 cloves garlic, 1 pinch cumin, 1 tsp sweet paprika powder, 1 bunch smooth parsley, 5 tbsp olive oil, 3 tbsp sesame paste, 3 lemons, salt

Preparation
Soak the chickpeas in cold water for 12 hours.

Then cook for 1 hour until soft. The pressure cooker is faster (only 5 minutes). Drain and set aside water.

Puree all Ingredients from chickpeas to salt in a blender. A smooth mass is to be created. If the mixture is too dry, add some of the cooking water.

Finally stir in the sesame paste and lemon juice.

Put it in the fridge. Ready!

Fun Fact
Hummus is an oriental speciality made from pureed chickpeas, sesame mush (Tahina), olive oil, lemon juice, salt and spices such as garlic and cumin.

Paprika Humus

Ingredients
250 g chickpeas, 3 red peppers or 1 glass of roasted peppers, 2 cloves of garlic, 3 tbsp lemon juice, 1 tbsp olive oil, 60 ml sesame paste, 2 pinches salt, 2 pinches pepper, ½ TL cumin, cayenne pepper

Preparation
Soak the chickpeas in cold water for 12 hours.

Rinse the chickpeas and boil them in unsalted water until al dente.

Grill the peppers in the oven at the highest setting all around and let them turn black. Then pour into a freezer bag, seal it and let it cool in the freezer compartment. Then remove the black skin.

Now pour all Ingredients into a blender and puree them.

Fill into glasses, pour a little olive oil over it and close.

Mushroom Dip

Ingredients
300 g white mushrooms, 100 g round grain rice, 50 g potatoes, 2 tsp oil, 200 ml vegetable broth, 1 clove of garlic, pepper, paprika powder, saltwater

Preparation
Peel the potatoes and cook them in a little salted water until soft.

Boil the rice in the vegetable stock, then turn down the stove to the lowest setting. Cover and leave to stand for about 30 - 35 minutes.

Clean and chop the mushrooms and sauté in oil together with the crushed clove of garlic.

Refine with pepper and paprika and stir until the liquid has evaporated from the mushrooms.

Now add the potatoes and the rice and puree everything.

Possibly season to taste.

Creamy-aromatic Ginger-Sesame Dip

Ingredients
200 g silk tofu, 1 tbsp sesame paste, 1 tbsp peanut butter, 1-piece ginger (approx. 4 cm), 1 clove garlic, 1 tsp agave syrup, 1 tsp dark Chinese vinegar, 2 tbsp soy sauce

Preparation
Puree all Ingredients. Carefully add the soy sauce bit by bit. The special aroma of Chinese vinegar contributes greatly to the aroma of the dip.

If the consistency is still too firm at the end despite sufficient saltiness, you can also carefully add a little water.

Greek Fava from Chickpeas

Ingredients
250 g dried chickpeas, 1 m. large red onion, 150 ml olive oil, 1/2 m. large onion, some parsley, salt and pepper

Preparation
Soak the chickpeas in cold water for 12 hours.

Place cold water in a saucepan, add softened chickpeas and half a peeled onion, bring to the boil and add salt.

Reduce the temperature and let the chickpeas simmer gently for about 90 minutes.

Drain and puree the chickpeas (without half the onion!) with about half the oil, adding salt and pepper if necessary.

Place the dish on a deep plate, pour the rest of the oil over it and sprinkle with some onion rings and parsley.

Tip: Can be enjoyed lukewarm or cold.

Fun Fact
Fava is a yellow puree that is sprinkled with plenty of olive oil and onion rings, usually served lukewarm. Hummus may look similar to Fava and have the same consistency, but it is not the original. Fava comes from the island of Santorini in the Cyclades. There Fava is as common as spaghetti in Italy.

Fava from red Lentils

Ingredients
250 g red lentils, 3 garlic cloves, 3 tablespoons olive oil, 3 spring onions, salt and pepper

Preparation
Wash the lenses thoroughly.

Add enough water, lentils and peeled garlic cloves, salt, cook for about 30 minutes until soft and drain through a sieve. Collect the cooking water.

Remove the garlic cloves as desired.

Now puree the lentils with the olive oil. Depending on the desired consistency, add a little more of the collected cooking water.

Season the Fava with salt and pepper and garnish with the finely sliced spring onions.

Tip: The Fava can be eaten lukewarm or cold.

Oriental white Bean Paste

Ingredients
240 g canned white beans, 2 cloves garlic, 4 tbsp olive oil, 5 peppercorns, 1 tsp coriander, 1 tsp mustard seed, 1 tsp cumin, 1 pinch cinnamon powder, 1 tsp sugar, 2 tbsp lemon juice, 1 dried chilli pepper, 3 tbsp coriander green, salt and pepper, abrasion of a lemon peel, some stock

Preparation
Drain the beans and rinse with water.

Roast coriander, pepper, mustard and cumin in a pan without oil until the spices begin to smell intensely.

Now grind the spices with a mortar or a food processor.

Put the olive oil in a pan and fry the coarsely chopped garlic and the chopped chilli pepper on a low heat until they are slightly brown.

Add the contents of the pan and the lemon juice to the beans and puree. When mashing, add some stock until the desired consistency is achieved.

Stir in the remaining Ingredients and spices and season with salt, pepper, lemon juice and sugar.

Tomato-Oregano-Pesto

Ingredients
250 g tomatoes preserved in oil, 50 g fresh oregano, 4 tablespoons tomato paste, 250 ml olive oil, 3 cloves garlic, sea salt and black pepper

Preparation
Chop the dried tomatoes, oregano and garlic.

Put the Ingredients together with the tomato paste and the olive oil into the blender and puree everything to a paste. Season with salt and pepper and season to taste.

Pour the pesto into small glasses and pour in some olive oil. Keep the glasses in the fridge.

Fun Fact
Pesto is a pasty, uncooked sauce that is usually eaten with noodles in Italian cuisine.

Trofie or Trenette are chosen especially in the region of origin. The most famous, Pesto alla genovese, contains in its original form basil mixed with pine nuts, enriched with garlic and olive oil, as well as cheese.

Guacamole

Ingredients
2 ripe avocados, 1 small onion, 1 jalapeño or fresh chilli pepper, 1 tomato, 1 juice of a lime, salt

Preparation
Peel and core the two avocados and crush or puree them with a fork in a bowl.

Add the lime juice immediately to prevent the avocado from turning brown.

Cut the onion, jalapeño or fresh chilli and tomato with peel into very small cubes and mix into the avocado mixture. If the tomato is too watery, let it drip off a little.

Season the guacamole with salt.

Fun Fact
Guacamole is an avocado dip from Mexican cuisine. There it is eaten, for example, with taquitos, tortilla chips.

Avocado - Mustard - Dip

Ingredients
1 ripe avocado, 1 garlic clove, 1 tbsp olive oil, 1 tbsp medium hot mustard, 3/4 tsp salt, 1 tsp lemon juice, some pepper

Preparation
Remove the seeds from the avocado and spoon out the flesh with a spoon and place in a bowl.

Press the garlic clove, add olive oil, mustard, salt, lemon juice and pepper and crush or puree everything with a fork.

Tip: Tastes very delicious on fresh bread.

Fun Fact
The avocado fruit, actually a berry, is pear-shaped to oval, depending on the species its leathery outer shell is medium to dark green (which has earned it the name alligator pear); inside there is a core about the size of a golf ball. The flesh is greenish yellow to golden yellow and oxidises to a dark colour when exposed to air - this can be prevented by rapid addition of antioxidants such as ascorbic acid contained in lemon juice. Certain varieties are also used for medicinal purposes (for example as a bactericide and against diarrhoea, or for controlled weight gain due to the high fat content of about 25%).

Auberginepuree

Ingredients
2 m. large fresh aubergines, 4 cloves garlic, 75 ml olive oil, 2 tbsp red wine vinegar, 1/2 tbsp sugar, some salt, black pepper

For the garnish:
A few black olives (black, pitted and chopped), some parsley, some olive oil.

Preparation
Preheat the oven to 190°C.

Prick the aubergines all around with a fork. Place on a baking tray oiled with olive oil and bake for approx. 1 hour until the skin is wrinkled and the meat soft.

Then let the aubergines cool down a little and peel. Cut the aubergines into small pieces with a knife and put them in a bowl with the garlic.

Using a wooden spoon, alternately stir in the oil and vinegar and finally add the sugar, salt and pepper.

Can be served cold or lukewarm, sprinkled with chopped olives and parsley.

South African Mango - Chili - Relish

Ingredients
1 ripe mango, 1 red hot chilli pepper, 1 ginger root, approx. 1-2 cm, 1 lime or lemon, 3 mint stalks, salt and pepper, a little agave syrup or syrup

Preparation
Peel the mango. Remove the flesh from the stone and cut into small pieces.

Remove the seeds from the chillies and chop into small pieces.

Peel and finely grate the ginger.

Pluck the mint leaves from the stalk and chop them into small pieces.

Squeeze the lime.

Puree all Ingredients in a blender to a pulp.

Season with agave syrup or syrup, salt and pepper and refrigerate.

Aubergine onion spread

Ingredients
½ medium aubergine, 1 onion, 2-3 tablespoons margarine, some pepper and salt

Preparation
Dice the aubergine and peeled onion very finely.

Melt and salt the margarine in a pan.

Steam the aubergine cubes and the onion cubes while stirring until the onions are glassy and the aubergines soft.

Season to taste with salt and pepper.

Allow to cool and then puree.

Wild garlic Pesto

Ingredients
1-2 hands full of wild garlic, ½ T walnuts, salt and pepper, olive oil

Preparation
Crush all Ingredients in a mixer.

Depending on taste, add plenty or little olive oil.

Tip: Either eat immediately or fill into boiled, lockable glasses and cover with some olive oil.

Fun Fact
The bear's garlic is a well-known vegetable, spice and medicinal plant. Although the plant is completely edible, it is mainly the leaves that are used, often with the stems, fresh as a spice, for dip sauces, herb butter and pesto or generally as vegetables in the spring kitchen. Bear's garlic gimchi produced by lactic acid fermentation can also be kept for many months.

The heat changes the sulphurous substances, causing the wild garlic to lose much of its characteristic taste. Therefore, it is usually mixed raw and cut into small pieces with salads or other dishes. In spring, bear's garlic can also replace chives or onion.

Béchamel sauce for Lasagne

Ingredients
1 l soymilk, 3 tbsp almond paste, 1 tbsp starch, 1 pr nutmeg, vegetable bouillon powder for one liter

Preparation
Pour the soymilk (up to 1/3 cup) into a pot, mix with the vegetable stock powder and almond paste and heat.

Mix the starch with the remaining 1/3 cup of soymilk.

Stir in everything together with nutmeg and bring to the boil briefly.

Currysauce

Ingredients
2 tbsp margarine, 2 tbsp flour, 1 ½ T soymilk, 2 tsp curry, salt

Preparation
Melt margarine with curry.

Stir in the flour until both have mixed.

To prevent lumps from forming, slowly add the soymilk while stirring.

Bring to the boil.

Season to taste with salt.

Tip: Tastes good with noodles, cereals, fried meats, vegetables, potatoes and more.

Peanutsauce

Ingredients
2 tsp margarine, 1 tbsp peanut butter, 1 tbsp flour, 2 tsp lemon juice, 1/2 cup soymilk, some salt

Preparation
Melt the margarine in a pot, add the flour and stir until smooth.

Add the peanut butter and stir until smooth.

Stir in the soymilk and season to taste with lemon juice and salt.

Bring to the boil while stirring until the sauce takes on a creamy consistency.

Tip: Tastes good with noodles or rice with vegetables or pulses.

Spring Soybean curd Cheese

Ingredients
300 g tofu, 1/2 cup soymilk, 3 tbsp linseed oil, 3 tbsp lemon juice, 1 teaspoon salt, 1/2 teaspoon white pepper, 1 bunch spring onions or ½ leek, 1 bowl cress or ½ bunch smooth parsley

Preparation
Mix the tofu with the soymilk, lemon juice, oil and spices in a tall container and puree well until the mixture has a creamy consistency.

Using a spoon, fold the spring onions (or leek) cut into small rings and the cut cress (or chopped smooth parsley) into the soybean quark.

Leave to stand in the fridge for 30 minutes.

Low Fat Potato Mayo

Ingredients
1 boiled potato, 1/3 cup soymilk, 2 teaspoons vinegar or lemon juice, 1 teaspoon mustard, 1 garlic clove, salt

Preparation
Peel the potato and garlic.

Puree all Ingredients with a blender jar.

Season to taste with salt.

Ketchup

Ingredients
200 g tomato paste, 200 ml vegetable broth, 1/3 T sugar, 3 tbsp vinegar, 1-2 tsp herb salt, 1 tsp paprika powder, some pepper

Preparation
Mix all Ingredients.

Pour into a pot, cook for 3 minutes and pour into a screw glass.

Keep in fridge.

Brownsauce

Ingredients
3 tablespoons olive oil, 3 tablespoons flour, 600 ml vegetable broth, 3 tablespoons soy sauce, salt and pepper

Preparation
Heat olive oil, add flour and brown for about 3-4 minutes while stirring.

Stir in the vegetable stock carefully and simmer for 10 minutes.

Flavour with soy sauce, salt and pepper.

Nut Bolognese

Ingredients
150 g nuts, finely chopped, 1 onion, 2 cloves garlic, 750 g fresh tomatoes, 2 tbsp chopped oregano, 2 tbsp chopped thyme, salt and pepper, some oil, possibly chilli powder, tomato paste or Ajvar if necessary

Preparation
Roast the finely chopped nuts without fat in a pan.

Cut the onion and garlic into small pieces and sauté in the oil in a saucepan.

Cut the tomatoes (peel if necessary) into small cubes.

Add nuts, herbs and tomatoes to the onions and garlic in the pot and simmer for 15 minutes.

Add some tomato paste or Ajvar as needed. The amount depends on how liquid the sauce is.

Season with salt, pepper and possibly chilli and simmer for another 10 minutes.

Dried Tomatoes - Nut - Pesto

Ingredients
8 dried tomatoes, 1 handful of peeled and roasted hazelnuts, 2 cloves of garlic, 100 ml olive oil, basil to taste, some smooth fresh parsley, some pepper, if necessary, pine nuts

Preparation
Cut the garlic and tomatoes into small pieces and puree. Crush the hazelnuts in a mortar and add to the tomato paste above.

Slowly add the olive oil and mix well until a creamy paste is obtained.

Cut the basil leaves and parsley into small pieces and mix in. Season to taste with pepper if necessary and leave to stand for at least 2 hours.

If you like, add some more roasted pine nuts.

Fun Fact
Pesto is a pasty, uncooked sauce that is usually served with pasta in Italian cuisine. Trofie or Trenette are chosen especially in the region of origin. The most famous, Pesto alla genovese, contains in its original form basil mixed with pine nuts, enriched with garlic and olive oil, as well as cheese.

Mushroom - Pesto

Ingredients
3 garlic cloves, 1 small onion, 2 spring onions, 50 ml olive oil, 250 g brown mushrooms, 1 handful walnuts, 2 fresh red chillies, 1 cup vegetable stock, 3 tbsp dried tomato, ½ bunch smooth parsley, salt

Preparation
Clean the mushrooms and cut them into small pieces. Peel and chop the onion and garlic into small pieces.

Fry onion and garlic in a large pan in a little olive oil, add spring onions (cut into fine rings) and fry briefly.

Add the mushrooms (with stems), chilli and dried tomatoes and fry gently for about 5 minutes until soft.

Parsley and walnuts in the very small chop. Add the contents of the pan, the rest of the olive oil, the broth and puree everything. Season to taste with salt.

Tip: Tastes good with spaghetti or macaroni and freshly grated Parmesan cheese.

Fun Fact
Pesto is a pasty, uncooked sauce that is usually served with pasta in Italian cuisine. Trofie or Trenette are chosen especially in the region of origin. The most famous, Pesto alla genovese, contains in its original form basil mixed with pine nuts, enriched with garlic and olive oil, as well as cheese.

Walnutpaste

Ingredients
200 g walnuts, 75 g breadcrumbs, 1 1/2 tbsp ground turmeric, 2 tbsp hot paprika powder, 1 tbsp harissa spice paste, 1 lemon, the juice thereof, 50 ml pomegranate syrup, 250 ml sunflower oil, 2 teaspoons salt

Preparation
Chop the walnuts very finely and mix with all other **Ingredients** (except the oil).

Stir the mixture well until all the Ingredients have mixed well.

Gradually add the oil and work in.

Leave the paste to brew overnight in the refrigerator. Possibly add some oil the next day.

Serve cold with flat bread, for example.

Tapenade

Ingredients
200 g green or/ and black olives, ½ lemon, the juice thereof, 1 bunch of smooth parsley, 1 small red onion, 1 clove of garlic, 50 g ground almonds, herb salt, possibly some olive oil

Preparation
Mix olives with parsley, garlic, onion and lemon juice in a mixer until a paste is formed. If you do not have a blender at hand, the Ingredients can also be cut into small pieces and crushed with a fork.

Then add the finely ground almonds and season to taste with herb salt.

Depending on the consistency, refine the tapenade with olive oil.

Fun Fact
The tapenade is an olive paste from the southern French cuisine. Main Ingredients are pitted olives, anchovies and capers (tapenos). It is used as a spread or dip sauce.

If the word is used incorrectly, other spreads are also referred to as tapenade, such as tomato tapenade, which is based on dried tomatoes and does not require olives.

Quince - Horseradish - Chutney

Ingredients
1 kg quince, 300 ml dry white wine, ½ litres apple juice, 180 g sugar, 30 g grated horseradish, 1 chili pepper, 1 lemon, the juice thereof, 1 tablespoon balsamic vinegar, 1 tablespoon sea salt with herbs, white pepper

Preparation
Wipe the quinces with a dry kitchen towel and wash.

Peel, quarter and core the quinces and cut them into even slices.

Cook the white wine and the apple juice.

Caramelise the sugar.

Add the mixture of apple juice and white wine.

Add the quinces and cook until soft.

Remove half of the quinces and chop coarsely. Then put it aside as an insert.

Puree the remaining quinces.

Add the horseradish, the chilli pepper and the quince slices, bring to the boil and remove from the heat.

Flavour with lemon juice, vinegar, herb salt and pepper.

Tip: Fill the chutney into preheated glasses and close immediately.

Aubergine cream with Sesamepaste

Ingredients
500 g eggplants, 4 tbsp sesame paste, 3 garlic cloves, 3 tbsp olive oil, lemon juice, salt and pepper, chilli flakes

Preparation
Preheat the oven to the highest setting.

Place the aubergines, cut in half and pricked with a fork, with the cut side down, on a grid in the oven and bake for about 30 minutes.

If the eggplants are soft, take them out of the oven.

Spoon out the flesh of the aubergines.

Peel the garlic cloves, crush them coarsely and puree them with the flesh of the aubergines, sesame paste and olive oil.

Then season the cream with lemon juice, salt and pepper.

Tip: Place in a bowl and sprinkle with chilli flakes.

Salsa

Ingredients
5 peeled tomatoes, 2 red peppers, 2 green peppers, 3 m. large onions, 2 chilli peppers, 1 lemon, 1 tbsp. salt, 2 tbsp. sugar

Preparation
Place the washed and diced vegetables and all other **Ingredients** in a pot without a lid and cook for about 1.5 hours at medium heat until the salsa has a creamy substance. Stir several times.

The amount of sugar, salt and chilli, can be changed at will.

Fun Fact
Salsa is the Spanish word for sauce. In the German-speaking world, the term salsa is mostly used to refer to Preparations typical of Mexican cuisine that are seasoned with chilli and pepper. Although it is often used cold as a dip (e.g. for tortillas and tacos), it is usually cooked during production. An exception is Pico de gallo, a traditional salsa whose Ingredients are exclusively mixed and served raw.

Gypsysauce

Ingredients
1 red pepper, 1 onion, 1 packet of tomatoes, 1 tablespoon tomato puree, olive oil for frying, salt and pepper, sugar, curry, paprika

Preparation
Peel the peppers into strips and the onion and cut into rings.

Brown both in olive oil.

Briefly fry the tomato paste with a little sugar and deglaze with the strained tomatoes.

Season to taste with the spices.

Cook the sauce at low heat for about 15 minutes.

Aioli

Ingredients
6 large cloves of garlic, 50 ml olive oil, 50 ml sunflower oil, some coarse sea salt, possibly lemon juice

Preparation
Puree the garlic cloves with the sea salt and then add alternating drops of olive oil and sunflower oil. Stir all the time.

Season to taste with lemon juice if desired.

Tip: You should prepare it exactly as described above, otherwise it will not succeed. If you are using a hand purifier, you should get help. One purées and one drips the oil alternately. If you have made it flawless, this side dish is similar in consistency to mayonnaise.

Fun Fact
Aioli is a cold cream from the Mediterranean area, which consists mainly of garlic, olive oil and salt. Aioli can be served as a starter, side dish or as a side dish with bread, flat bread or baguette.

Apple - Figs - Chutney

Ingredients

1 kg apples, 50 g ginger, 150 g sugar, 50 g ground almonds, 1 tablespoon yellow mustard powder, 100 ml honey vinegar, 3 fresh figs, some salt

Preparation

Peel, quarter, core and dice the apples.

Peel the ginger root and cut into pieces.

Mix apples and ginger root with sugar, almonds, mustard powder, salt and vinegar, bring to the boil and simmer for about 30 minutes.

Then wash and skin the figs and cut them into small pieces. Put the figs in the pot and let them simmer for about 15 minutes.

Fill the chutney hot and boiling into closable jars, close immediately and place on the lid for 5 minutes.

Sesamesauce

Ingredients
300 g sesame paste, 300 g water, 1 large lemon, 2 cloves of garlic, coarsely chopped, 1 handful of smooth parsley, salt, cumin

Preparation
Place the sesame paste, water, lemon juice, garlic and parsley in a tall container and puree.

Season to taste with salt and crushed cumin.

Cool and enjoy.

Tip: The sesame sauce tastes great with mixed salad, pasta or rice.

Desserts

Chocolate Mousse

Ingredients
1/2 packet Seidentofu, 75 g vegan dark chocolate, 1/2 tbsp rum, 1 packet vanilla sugar, possibly some birch sugar, grated coconut

Preparation
Puree the tofu very well in a blender.

Now melt the chocolate in a pot and add it with the remaining Ingredients to the tofu (with sugar or without sugar, you decide) and puree the whole again well.

Pour the mousse into a bowl or glasses and place in the fridge.

Before serving, you may, if you like, decorate the mousse with grated coconut.

Fun Fact
Mousse au Chocolat is a classic French dessert made of dark chocolate.

Sweet Pancakes

Ingredients
1 cup vegan clear or cloudy apple juice (make sure that the apple juice is not made with gelatine), 2 teaspoons baking powder, 2 cups wheat flour, 2 teaspoons brown syrup or sugar, 1 cup soymilk, 1 pinch salt, vegetable fat, for frying

Preparation
Mix all Ingredients with a whisk or mixer to a smooth dough.

Heat some fat in a pan, add enough dough with a ladle and fry on both sides on medium heat.

Tip: Serve as desired with icing sugar, fruits, jam, nut nougat cream or similar.

Tiramisu

Ingredients
For the dough:
120 g flour, 80 g sugar cube, 3 tbsp sunflower oil, 125 ml water, 2 tsp baking powder, 300 ml cold strong coffee, 50 ml Amaretto

For the cream:
250 ml soy cream, 150 ml water, 80 g sugar, 50 g semolina, untreated lemon, of which the grated zest, 1 packet vanilla sugar, 2 tsp cinnamon, 2 tbsp amaretto, 1 pinch salt, 120 g margarine

Preparation
Starting with the dough:
Mix flour, sugar, oil, water and baking powder with the hand mixer and spread the mixture on a baking tray (baking tin approx. 20 cm x 30 cm or half baking tray and baking paper).

Bake the dough for approx. 20 minutes at 180°C and then let it cool.

After cooling, cut into pieces the size of a sponge cake.

Continue geht's with the cream:
Put the soy cream, water, sugar and semolina in a saucepan and bring to the boil while stirring, then simmer for 3 minutes.

Remove from the heat and continue stirring well to prevent clotting.

Now add the lemon zest, vanilla sugar, cinnamon, 2 tablespoons amaretto and salt and mix well.

Then place the mixture in the refrigerator for 1 hour. In the meantime, however, you should stir it from time to time.

Finally add the margarine and stir again until the mixture is creamy. If the margarine still lumps, just puree it.

Mix the coffee with the 50 ml Amaretto and put it into a flat bowl.

Dip the strips of sponge cake into it and layer them on the bottom of a smaller dish (approx. 20 x 20 cm).

Over it half of the cream give, then again a layer of sponge cake and finally again cream.

Sprinkle with cocoa powder and refrigerate for 5 hours.

Fun Fact
The Tiramisu (literally "pull me up") is a dessert from Veneto, known far beyond its place of origin.

Strawberry Ice Cream

Ingredients
100-150 g strawberries, 2-3 tsp cane sugar, 3-4 tbsp soymilk

Preparation
Remove the green of the strawberries, wash and cut them into small pieces.

Now freeze the strawberries overnight.

Take the strawberries out of the freezer and thaw them for about 15 minutes.

Now puree the strawberries with the remaining Ingredients.

Strawberry Shake

Ingredients
200g strawberries, 2 cups soymilk, 1 banana, 1-2 tablespoons sugar

Preparation
Puree all Ingredients except two strawberries.

Fill into two glasses.

Cut the two remaining strawberries into pieces and place them on the edge of the glass.

Peanut Cream

Ingredients
2 tbsp peanut butter, 3-4 tbsp soymilk, 4 dried dates, 1 tbsp thick fruit juice, 1 tbsp lemon juice

Preparation
Mix peanut butter, soymilk, fruit syrup and lemon juice to a uniform cream.

Cut the dates into small cubes and sprinkle them over the cream.

Semolina Porridge

Ingredients
2 cups soymilk, 2 tbsp sugar, 1 pinch salt, ½ T Soft wheat semolina, sugar if you like, cinnamon if you like

Preparation
Bring the soymilk, sugar and salt to the boil in a saucepan.

Now add the semolina and bring to the boil while stirring.

Then let simmer for 8-10 minutes at low heat, stirring more often.

Fill the porridge into plates or bowls, sprinkle with sugar or cinnamon.

Tip: You can also serve the semolina porridge with compote or fresh fruit.

Hazelnut Ice Cream

Ingredients
1 cup soy cream, 2 tbsp hazelnut puree, 3 tbsp maple syrup or thick fruit juice, 1 tbsp margarine

Preparation
First melt the margarine and then mix thoroughly with the other Ingredients.

Freeze for about an hour.

After this hour, stir the ice thoroughly and freeze for another 45 minutes.

Stir thoroughly again.

And because it was so beautiful, you freeze the ice again. This time for a few hours or overnight.

Allow to defrost for 20-30 minutes.

Crush the ice coarsely with a fork.

Puree with a hand blender to crush the ice crystals, adding a little soymilk if necessary.

Tip: Of course, other nut mash such as almond, cashew kernel or peanut mash can also be used.

Chocolate Ice Cream

Ingredients
1 can coconut milk, 1 bar chocolate, 70-80 % cocoa, 1 bar chocolate, 60 % cocoa, ½ cup sugar, ½ TL vanilla powder, 1 pinch salt, 5 TL cocoa powder, some almond milk, alternatively also oat milk

Preparation
Break both chocolate bars into small pieces and melt them in a water bath while stirring constantly.

Mix 5-6 teaspoons of cocoa powder with almond milk in a cup until a thin paste is obtained.

Add the cocoa mass to the melted chocolate, stir in the vanilla powder, sugar, coconut milk and salt, mix well and refrigerate for 2-3 hours.

Then pour into the ice-cream maker and enjoy after about 40-50 minutes.

If you don't have an ice machine, it's fine. Then you just do the same thing as with hazelnut ice cream:

Freeze the ice for about an hour.

After this hour, stir the ice thoroughly and freeze for another 45 minutes.

Stir thoroughly again.

And because it was so beautiful, you freeze the ice again. This time for a few hours or overnight.

Allow to defrost for 20-30 minutes.

Crush the ice coarsely with a fork.

Puree with a hand blender to crush the ice crystals, possibly adding a little almond milk.

Fruit Ice Cream with Tofu

Ingredients
500 g fruits (e.g. strawberries, raspberries, kiwi, apricots etc.), 4 tbsp lemon juice, fresh or bottled, 4 tbsp maple syrup, 100 g tofu, 100 ml soymilk vanilla

Preparation
Drain the berries after washing and remove seeds if necessary.

Then put the fruits into the blender and put the other Ingredients into the blender as well.

Now mix vigorously.

Pour the fruit pulp into a flat dish and let it freeze in the freezer for 1 hour.

After this hour, stir the whole thing with a whisk and put it in the freezer again for 3 hours.

You can also put the mixture in an ice cream machine and let it freeze for 30 minutes.

Bananas - Coconut - Ice Cream

Ingredients
50 g grated coconut, 2 bananas, 100 ml coconut milk, 1 tablespoon maple syrup, some lime juice

Preparation
Place the grated coconut on a baking tray and roast in the oven at 200°C for just a few minutes. Please be careful, because this is very fast.

Now cut the bananas into thick slices and freeze them for an hour. Then chop coarsely in a blender.

Add the coconut milk, maple syrup and lime juice to the blender and mix in 1-2 minutes to a smooth mixture (the mixture seems to flocculate first, but then becomes smooth after a while).

Fold in roasted coconut flakes and enjoy immediately.

Banana Ice Cream

Ingredients
2 almost overripe bananas, with already black spots, 4 tbsp soymilk, 2 tsp sugar, 1 tsp almond paste optional

Preparation
Peel the bananas, cut them into slices and freeze them overnight.

Allow to defrost for 10 minutes and puree with the remaining Ingredients.

Coconut Pudding

Ingredients
400ml coconut milk, 2 go. tbsp corn starch, 2 tbsp sugar

Preparation
Stir the corn starch with a little coconut milk until smooth.

Heat the rest of the coconut milk with the sugar, stir in the corn starch with a whisk and bring to the boil.

Put into cold rinsed dessert bowls and leave to cool.

Tip: The coconut milk is made from the white solid part of the coconut, not to be confused with the coconut milk, the turbid liquid inside the nut.

Crepes

Ingredients
250 g flour, 250 ml soymilk, 250 ml mineral water, 2 tbsp oil, 1 pinch salt, 1 tbsp vanilla sugar

Preparation
Mix all Ingredients to a dough without lumps and let rest for 2 hours covered. Or even overnight.

Make sure that the dough is as thin as possible. You may want to add a little more soymilk.

Then fry in a pan spread with a little oil, or with the Crêpes-Maker wafer-thin crêpes.

Fun Fact
A crepe, is a Breton form of pancake. Crêpes are very thin and are traditionally baked on a round, cast-iron plate, the so-called crêpière. To make the crêpes thin and even, the liquid dough is quickly spread with a dough rake. The dough is usually tasteless or prepared with little salt. It is more liquid compared to German pancake dough.

In Brittany, crêpes are generally topped with sugar, jam, fresh fruit or nut nougat cream. One of the best-known variations is the Crêpe Suzette, in which the crêpes are soaked with the juice of fresh oranges or spread with orange jam.

Oranges - Spice Pancakes

Ingredients
100 g flour, 125 g wholemeal flour, 2 tsp baking powder, 1/2 tsp baking soda, 1/4 tsp ground cinnamon, 1/8 tsp ground nutmeg, 1 pinch ground cloves, 1 tsp grated orange peel (zest), 350 ml orange juice, 50 g raisins, oil, maple syrup

Preparation
Mix the flour, baking powder, baking soda and spices and add the orange peel, raisins and orange juice.

Mix everything quickly to a dough, but do not stir too long, just so that everything is just mixed.

Now pour the oil into a coated pan and heat it.

Now bake about 10 small pancakes from the dough and serve them with maple syrup. Or whatever else you'd like.

Banana Pancakes

Ingredients
200 g whole grain, 240 ml soymilk, 2 tbsp vanilla sugar, 2 Msp cardamom powder, 1 pinch salt, 1 large crushed banana, 2 tsp baking powder, 1 tbsp macadamia oil, some neutral oil for baking, maple syrup as required

Preparation
Mix all Ingredients carefully to a smooth dough.

Heat some neutral oil in a coated pan and bake small pancakes one after the other.

Results in about 14 pieces.

Wild berries - Smoothie

Ingredients
350 ml orange juice, 1 banana, 450 g deep-frozen mixed berries, 2 oranges

Preparation
Freeze the bananas for an hour.

Put the orange juice, frozen banana slices and the wild berries into a blender or food processor and puree.

Spread the smoothie over 2 glasses.

Fun Fact
Smoothies is a US-American term for so-called whole fruit drinks. They are also sold as finished products. In contrast to conventional fruit juices, smoothies process the whole fruit down to the peel and seeds. The basis of the smoothies is therefore the fruit pulp or fruit puree, which, depending on the recipe, is mixed with juices to obtain a creamy consistency. Smoothies are available in many different variations. Many smoothies consist only of fruit, i.e. fruit flesh and direct juices. The banana often forms a basic ingredient.

Chocolates - Peanutbutter - Tofu - Pudding

Ingredients
250 g silk tofu, 170 g sugar, 130 g creamy peanut butter, 180 ml water, 230 g vegan dark chocolate, 1 vanilla pod, scraped out pulp of it

For the garnish:
possibly whipped soy cream
possibly chocolate chips

Preparation
In a small pot, boil the sugar with the water and simmer, stirring occasionally, until the sugar has completely dissolved.

To cool, take the pot off the stove.

Now pour all Ingredients (except the soy cream and the chocolate chips) into a blender and mix until it has a homogeneous consistency.

Spread over six dessert bowls and refrigerate for at least one hour.

Serve garnished with cream and chocolate chips as desired.

Tofu Fruit Cream

Ingredients
400 g soft tofu, 360 g unsweetened apple sauce, unsweetened, 2 m. large ripe bananas, 1/2 tsp real ground vanilla, 2 tbsp freshly squeezed lemon juice

For decoration
1 small ripe banana, sliced

Optional
as required soymilk or soy cream, as required concentrated juice, agave concentrated juice

Preparation
Puree the banana with the lemon juice and vanilla.

Add the unsweetened apple sauce and mash again briefly.

Finally add the tofu in cubes and purée until a uniform cream is obtained.

Divide the tofu fruit cream into 4 portion bowls and garnish with the banana slices.

Tip: The tofu fruit cream is suitable as dessert (4 portions), protein-rich breakfast or snack.

Cashew Cream

Ingredients
200 g cashew nuts, 800 ml apple juice, 2 tbsp sunflower oil, sugar as required, vanilla flavour as required

Preparation
Add the cashew nuts to the apple juice and bring to the boil.

Then reduce the heat and simmer for about 5 to 10 minutes.

Cover the apple juice and nuts and leave the pot to cool for a few hours or overnight.

Take out the cashew nuts with a fork and puree them with the oil. Please make sure that you take as little apple juice as possible with you when removing the nuts.

Then season to taste with sugar and/or vanilla flavouring.

Tip: This cream tastes particularly good with fruit salads, but can also be used as a dessert cream or spread.

Wholemeal spelt Waffles

Ingredients
2 tablespoons maple syrup or thick fruit juice, 50 g vegan margarine, 1 pinch salt, 250 ml sparkling mineral water, 200 g spelt flour, 1 teaspoon cinnamon

Preparation
Mix flour, salt, cinnamon.

Mix the margarine with the maple syrup or thick fruit juice, the wholemeal flour, the flour-salt-cinnamon mixture and the mineral water to a thick dough and let it swell for about 45-60 minutes.

Then stir again.

Preheat the waffle iron and bake four waffles one after the other.

Microwave Cup Cake

Ingredients
4 tbsp flour, 6 tbsp soymilk, 1 tbsp sugar, 1 tbsp cocoa powder, ½ Pck. vanilla sugar, ¼ tbsp baking powder, 1/2 tbsp lemon juice, 1 tbsp oil

Preparation
Mix all the Ingredients in a microwaveable cup until all the lumps have dissolved. Wipe the edge of the dough, otherwise it will crust during baking. Of course, you can also mix everything in a bowl and then add to the cup.

Place the cup in the microwave for 2 - 2 1/2 minutes at 700 watts. Attention, the cup is hot!

Tip: Try adding some soluble coffee powder to the dough.

Winter Orange Sorbet

Ingredients
¾ L freshly squeezed orange juice, 100 g cane sugar or diet sweetener, 1 teaspoon cinnamon, 1 teaspoon orange liqueur or tangerine liqueur, untreated orange, of which the grated peel (zest), n. B. mint leaves, orange fillets or orange slices for garnishing

Preparation
Strain 750 ml of freshly squeezed orange juice to remove the flesh, bring to the boil and mix with sugar or diet sweetness.

As soon as the sugar has dissolved, allow to cool.

Then add the cinnamon, the orange zest and the liqueur and mix together.

Now pour the mixture into a bowl and place in the freezer compartment of one.

Stir well every 20 minutes with a whisk so that no ice crystals form and all Ingredients are mixed well.

Depending on the cold of the freezer or freezer compartment, this must be repeated 6 to 8 times.

Serve in portion bowls, champagne bowls or cleaned, hollowed orange halves.

Tip: Garnish with mint and orange fillets or orange slices.

Fun Fact
Sorbet is the name for an ice-cold drink or a semi-frozen food made from fruit juice, fruit puree and sugar. There are also sorbets that contain champagne or wine instead of fruit juice. Classic is the lemon sorbet. The mass is stirred several times during

freezing to keep the sorbet smooth. Acid sorbets as a drink are often served as an intermediate course in a multi-course meal as they stimulate digestion and reduce the feeling of satiety. As half-frozen food they are a dessert. They also serve to neutralise between the aisles.

Vanilla pudding

Ingredients
500 ml soymilk, 40 g cornflour, 1 vanilla pod, 4 tablespoons sugar

Preparation
Place about 100 ml of 500 ml soymilk in a bowl and mix with the starch and sugar.

Scratch out the pulp of the vanilla pod.

Bring the rest of the soymilk to the boil in a saucepan with the vanilla pulp.

As soon as the milk boils, add the starch and stir vigorously with a whisk.

The whole thing has to boil up again and really thicken. But that's relatively quick.

Let the pudding cool and serve.

Halva

Ingredients
4 cups water, 2 cups sugar, ½ lemon, of which the grated peel (zest), 2 cloves, 1 teaspoon cinnamon powder, 2 cups semolina (soft wheat), ½ cup chopped almonds, ½ cup breadcrumbs, 1 cup neutral vegetable oil

Preparation
Put the water in a saucepan with the sugar, cloves, cinnamon and lemon zest and stir well so that the sugar dissolves.

Bring the sugar water mixture to the boil and let it boil at medium heat for about 10 minutes, so that a kind of thin syrup is formed. Stir again and again.

After about 10 minutes take the pot off the heat and remove the cloves and lemon peel.

Heat the neutral oil in another large pot and then add the soft wheat semolina.

Stir-fry until golden brown, then add breadcrumbs and chopped almonds and roast briefly.

Now remove the pot from the heat and gradually add the still warm syrup to the roasted semolina while stirring with a ladle. A solid paste must be produced.

Line a bowl or pudding tin with household foil and add the hot semolina porridge and press firmly. Leave to cool for at least an hour, then fall. Remove the foil and sprinkle with some cinnamon before serving.

Fun Fact
Halva is a confectionery speciality, which originates from India, Iran and Central Asia. Halva is also known

in the Near East, Southeast, Central and Eastern Europe.

Tofu Ragout with Pears and Rosemary

Ingredients
500 g packet natural tofu, 1 pear, 1 ½ packet soy cream, 3-4 tbsp apricot jam, oil or vegetable margarine, several sprigs fresh rosemary, salt, pepper, paprika, curry

Preparation
Cut the tofu into small cubes and fry them in a pan with olive oil or margarine.

Peel and eighth the pear and add to the tofu and fry briefly.

Remove the needles from 1 - 2 sprigs of rosemary and add them to the pan.

Now simmer for a few minutes with the lid closed.

Now add the soy cream and the apricot jam. Bring to the boil again briefly and season to taste with salt, pepper, curry and paprika powder.

Lemon Yoghurt

Ingredients
600 g natural soy yoghurt, 100 g agave syrup, ½ lemon, including the grated zest, 35 ml lemon juice, 5 drops essential lemon oil, 1 pinch sea salt, 50 g roasted and chopped almonds, lemon balm

Preparation
Mix all Ingredients with a whisk until the yoghurt is creamy.

Finally, sprinkle the almonds on top and garnish the yoghurt with lemon balm leaves.

Tip: Tastes like real yogurt.

Strawberrysorbet

Ingredients
500 g strawberries, 125 ml apple juice, 50 g icing sugar, 1 tablespoon lemon juice, some vanilla sugar as desired

Preparation
Wash and clean the strawberries.

Now put all the Ingredients in a bowl and puree everything.

Allow to cool in the refrigerator for about 1 hour.

Pour into the ice-cream maker, or pour into a flat bowl and place in the freezer. Stir frequently.

After approx. 3 hours puree again and serve.

Fun Fact
Sorbet is the name for an ice-cold drink or a semi-frozen food made from fruit juice, fruit puree and sugar. There are also sorbets that contain champagne or wine instead of fruit juice. Classic is the lemon sorbet. The mass is stirred several times during freezing to keep the sorbet smooth. Acid sorbets as a drink are often served as an intermediate course in a multi-course meal as they stimulate digestion and reduce the feeling of satiety. As half-frozen food they are a dessert. They also serve to neutralise between the aisles.

Sweet Spring Rolls

Ingredients
2 bananas, 1 mango, 1 kiwi, 1 teaspoon heaped vanilla sugar, 100 g fresh or frozen mixed berries, n. B. dough sheets for spring rolls, neutral oil to fry

Preparation
Defrost the spring roll leaves.

While the leaves thaw, cut the fruit into small cubes.

Now heat the vanilla sugar with a quarter of the berries in a pot until the berry cubes become slightly soft.

Remove one of the thawed spring roll leaves, halve it and heap some fruitfulness on one end (not too much, otherwise you can't make rolls out of it anymore).

Drive in and roll from the sides and then from below. Repeat the process with all the spring roll leaves until the berries are used up.

Heat the oil in a wok or frying pan and fry the rolls until they are lightly coloured.

Alternatively, you can fry them briefly.

Keep the rolls warm in the oven at 50 degrees.

Tip: The rolls also go well with vanilla ice cream or sauce.

Avocado - Sorbet

Ingredients
2 avocados, 3 oranges, 250 g sugar, 2 lemon(s), 400 g water, 1 pinch salt

Preparation
Peel and core the avocados.

Puree the meat of the avocados and sprinkle with the juice of the citrus fruits.

Now add sugar, salt and water and mix everything together.

Then pour the mass into the running ice cream machine. After approx. 30 - 45 minutes the ice is firm.

Then it can be placed in a pre-cooled container.

Tip: Fruit puree and biscuits go with it. It can be served as an exotic dessert, but also as an intermediate course!

Fun Fact
The non-alcoholic drink was transferred into other European languages around the 16th century through the mediation of Turkish (şerbet), in Italian as sorbetto, in French as sorbet. The form of Preparation of the drink also comes from the Middle East. It was served there only for special festive occasions. In Turkey, sorbet was then introduced at banquets as a small refreshment between several courses, but there and in Egypt it also became an everyday drink based on fruit syrup.

In the 17th century sorbet was a drink made of water, sugar and lemon in France. It was not until the 19th century that it could also describe a half-frozen dessert, which usually contained alcohol and was more sipped than eaten with a spoon.

Apricots - Marsala - Sorbet

Ingredients
1 kg fully ripe apricots, 200 ml Marsala (Italian wine). Instead of Marsala you can also take Madeira or red port wine. ½ Lemon, 250 g sugar

Preparation
Stone and quarter the apricots and place in a pot.

Bring to the boil with the Marsala, lemon juice and sugar.

Cover and simmer for approx. 3 minutes, then allow to cool.

Cut about 1/4 of the apricots into small cubes and set aside.

Add the remaining apricots to the pot and puree together with the contents.

Mix the apricot cubes you have put aside with the sorbet mixture and freeze them.

During the freezing process, carefully work through the mass 4 to 5 times with a rubber spatula so that no ice crystals form.

Fun Fact
Marsala is a liqueur wine that takes its name from the Sicilian port of Marsala, from where it is mainly exported to England.

Chocolate Banana Tofu Cream

Ingredients
400 g natural tofu (soft, but no silk tofu), 360 g unsweetened apple puree, 2 m. large ripe bananas, 2 tbsp freshly squeezed lemon juice, ½ TL vanilla pod, 4 tsp unsweetened cocoa powder

Ingredients for the decoration
1 small ripe banana, sliced, n.B. Soymilk or soy cream, n.B. agave syrup or stevia powder

Preparation
Puree the banana with the lemon juice and the pulp of the vanilla pod.

Add the apple sauce and the cocoa and mash again briefly.

Finally, cut the tofu into cubes and add them and purée until a homogeneous cream is obtained.

Tip: If you like the cream thin, you can stir in some more soymilk or soy cream as needed.

If you like it a little sweeter, you can sweeten the cream as you like. However, the fruit's own sweetness is perfectly sufficient.

Divide the chocolate banana tofu cream into 4 portion bowls and garnish with the banana slices.

Chocolate-Avocado Mousse

Ingredients
110 g coarsely hooked dark chocolate, 4 tbsp coconut cream, 1 ripe avocado, 1/2 tsp vanilla extract, some sea salt, 3 tbsp agave syrup, 1 tsp finely grated orange peel (zest), 1/2 tsp cayenne, chocolate shavings or coconut flakes

Preparation
Melt the chocolate in a water bath with the coconut cream until a creamy mass is formed and then allow to cool slightly.

Puree the chocolate mixture with the remaining Ingredients in the mixer to a creamy mousse.

Fill into dessert bowls and garnish with pomegranate seeds, chocolate shavings or coconut flakes.

Coconut Apricot Balls

Ingredients
220 g whole unsalted almonds, 260 g dried apricots, 2 tsp cinnamon, 2 tsp almond extract, 50 g coconut flakes

Preparation
Chop almonds, apricots, cinnamon and almond extract into small pieces in a food processor.

Roll the mixture into small balls with your hands and then roll the balls into the coconut flakes.

Results in approx. 16 balls.

Grilling

Grilled Vegetables

Ingredients
2 small courgettes, 1 red pepper, 1 yellow pepper, 1 onion, 2 potatoes, 120 ml olive oil, 2 cloves of garlic, 1 sprig thyme, 2 sprigs rosemary, salt

Preparation
Wash the vegetables.

Cut the zucchini and onion into slices about ½ cm thick.

Cut the peppers into quarters and slice or plane the potatoes thinly.

Put the olive oil in a bowl with crushed garlic, salt (to taste) and chopped herbs and mix.

Add the vegetables and leave to stand for about 2 hours. Stir well several times.

Brush a grill tray or aluminium foil with olive oil, spread the vegetables on top and grill until crispy, turning occasionally. Season to taste with salt.

Grilled Vegetables - Salad

Ingredients
2 red peppers, 2 yellow peppers, 2 onions, 1 courgette, 2 large carrots, 250 g mushrooms, 1 fennel, 6 cloves garlic, 3 tablespoons olive oil, 2 teaspoons salt, 3 tablespoons balsamic vinegar, 3 tablespoons walnut oil, possibly paprika powder and chili jibs

Preparation
First a hint: This salad is not grilled, but tastes fabulous with grilled.

Clean the vegetables and cut into bite-sized pieces, cut the onions into eighths.

Put the vegetables in a garbage bag and add the pressed garlic, olive oil and salt and shake well (sounds funny, but makes mixing easier). If required, chili flakes and paprika can also be added.

Place the vegetables on two baking trays lined with baking paper and bake in the oven at 200°C until the vegetables begin to brown.

Let the vegetables cool and then put them in a large bowl. Off

Make a marinade with balsamic vinegar and walnut oil and fold into the vegetables.

Oven Potato BBQ Style

Ingredients
3 large potatoes (approx. 300g per potato), 5 tablespoons rapeseed oil or sunflower oil, 2 cloves finely chopped garlic, 2 tablespoons BBQ spice mix, 1 teaspoon smoked salt

Preparation
Wash the potato thoroughly, brush off the skin if necessary and cut the potato into slices about 1 cm thick.

Preheat the oven to 180 degrees.

Mix oil, garlic, salt and spice mixture well and brush the potato slices on both sides with it. Place the potato slices on a baking tray lined with baking paper and place in the oven for approx. 30-35 minutes. Keep turning in between.

The potato slices are also excellent for grilling.

Tip: Excellent accompaniment to grilled, but also alone with a dip.

Fiery grilled Potato Skewers

Ingredients
600 g small early potatoes, 2 red chilli peppers, 2 cloves of garlic, 2 tablespoons olive oil, salt and pepper

Preparation
Cook the potatoes in their skins for about 10 minutes until almost cooked.

In the meantime, core the chillies. Dice the garlic and chilli very finely. Alternatively, you can also use dried chilli peppers.

Add the garlic, chilli, salt and pepper to the olive oil and the hot potatoes.

After cooling, stick on skewers and put on the hot grill from both sides for a few minutes.

Grilled Fennel

Ingredients
1 tuber large fennel, 2 large tomatoes, 2 large cloves of garlic, 2 sprigs rosemary, 2 sprigs thyme, 4 tablespoons olive oil, salt and pepper

Preparation
First you make 4 pieces of aluminum foil packs. To do this, take a sufficiently large piece of aluminium foil, place margarine in it and turn up the sides.

Then cut the fennel into thin slices and distribute into the 4 aluminium foils.

Cut the tomatoes into not too thin slices and spread on the fennel.

Cut the garlic cloves into fine slices and spread over the tomatoes.

Now season sufficiently with salt and pepper, halve the herb stalks and add to the vegetables.

Now distribute a spoonful of olive oil on each packet and seal the packets.

Place the well-sealed aluminium packets on the grill for approx. 15-20 minutes. Depending on how crunchy you like the fennel, try it out in between. Take a packet from the grill and see how firm the vegetables are.

Grilled Pita Bread

Ingredients
250 g flour, 250 ml lukewarm water, 10 g sugar, 2 tablespoons olive oil, 1 pck. dry yeast, some salt, some olive oil, for the bowl

Preparation
Put the sugar with the lukewarm water and the yeast in a bowl.

Leave to rise for about 15 minutes in a warm place.

Knead the flour with the yeast-water-sugar mixture slowly for 10 minutes in the food processor or by hand.

Now add some salt.

Place in a bowl spread with olive oil, cover with a cloth and leave in a warm place for another 30 minutes until the dough has doubled in volume.

Then knead the dough again briefly and divide into 10 - 12 pieces.

Roll out each piece to a flat cake. However, they should still be approx. ½ cm thick.

Allow the flat cakes to rise again for approx. 20 minutes and then grill on a medium heat for approx. 2 - 3 minutes per side.

Tofu - Skewers

Ingredients
250 g tofu, 10 tbsp soy sauce, 1 1/2 tsp tofu spice (available in health food stores), 1 tsp Garam-Masala spice mixture, 1 tsp ground ginger, 1 tsp chilli flakes, 150 g cherry tomatoes, paprika powder, pepper

Preparation
Cut the tofu into cubes (approx. 1.5 x 1.5 cm) and place in a bowl with a lid.

Then add the other Ingredients (except the tomatoes). Please use the paprika powder sparingly, otherwise it will become bitter when barbecued!

Close the lid and shake gently until all the Ingredients have mixed.

Let the tofu marinate for about 2 - 3 hours. Then skewer them alternately with the tomatoes on wooden skewers and finally grill them.

Grilled Asparagus

Ingredients
1 kg green or white fresh asparagus (250g per person), tarragon or sage, sesame oil, coarse sea salt, pepper

Preparation
Place the asparagus in a double layer of aluminium foil. Add a few drops of sesame oil to each of the asparagus spears. Now add tarragon or sage, coarse sea salt and pepper to the asparagus.

Wrap the aluminium foil into a "sweet" and close.

Then place on the hot grill and let grill for about 25 minutes. The asparagus is good if the asparagus packets can be bent easily.

Tip: Many different variations are possible here - e.g. drip some raspberry vinegar or balsamic vinegar onto the asparagus. Or grill with chilli and dried tomatoes, then season with sage and lemon.

Grill Marinade

Ingredients
1/2 t white wine vinegar, 2 tbsp rice wine, 1/2 t soy sauce, 2 tbsp water, 3 cloves of garlic, peeled and pressed, 2.5 cm large piece of ginger, peeled and finely chopped, 2 tbsp Chinese five-spice powder (to taste), 1/4 t olive oil, 2 tbsp molasses seasoning, green mixed herbs, fresh and chopped, freshly ground black pepper

Preparation
Place the desired grill food in an oven dish.

Mix all the Ingredients for the marinade in a medium bowl.

Pour the mixture over the grill until it is well coated.

Leave to stand for at least 24 hours, covered and cooled, if necessary, turn over from time to time.

Heat the grill.

Grill the marinated food for about 4-6 minutes from both sides, serve.

Grilled Mangoes with Raspberry Sauce

Ingredients
2 tbsp sugar, 1 tsp molasses, 2 tbsp freshly squeezed lime or lemon juice, 2 tsp fresh raspberries (or strawberries), 3-4 medium-sized mangoes, vegetable oil for the grill grid

Preparation
Mix sugar, molasses and lime juice well in a shallow bowl.

Add half of the raspberries and puree.

Peel the mangos and place them whole with one side in the raspberry sauce and let them rest at room temperature for about 45 minutes.

Grease the grill with the vegetable oil and heat the grill over medium heat.

Place the mangos with the marinated side down on the grill and put the marinade aside.

After 2 minutes turn the mangos over, then grill for another 6-8 minutes. Remove from the grill and pour half of the remaining marinade over it.

Stir the remaining raspberries into the remaining marinade and spread over the mangoes. Serve warm.

Tsatsiki

Ingredients
1 medium-sized cucumber, 2 tbsp vegan mayonnaise, 2 tbsp fresh mint, 1/4 tb freshly squeezed lemon juice, 4-6 cloves garlic, pressed or chopped, 1 tbsp freshly chopped dill cabbage (or 1 tsp dry dill tips), 1/8 tsp sea salt, 1/8 tsp freshly ground black pepper, 1 pinch cayenne pepper

Preparation
Grate the cucumber coarsely and place in a large bowl with the remaining Ingredients and mix well.

To make it taste a little sourer, please add more lemon juice. Serve cool.

Mediterranean hot Sauce

Ingredients
6 dried tomatoes, 2 t of different chilli peppers, sliced, 1/2 t of water (plus 2 tbsp. of the dried tomato water), 4 tbsp. freshly squeezed lime juice, 4 tsp. red wine or apple vinegar, 1/2 tsp. sea salt, 1 tsp. cane sugar, 2 cloves of garlic (optional), 1 tsp. smoked paprika powder (optional), 2 tbsp. olive oil (optional)

Preparation
Soak dried tomatoes in hot water for 15 minutes until soft.

Put the remaining Ingredients together with the soaking water of the tomatoes into a blender and stir until smooth.

Place the mixture in a glass and keep cool.

Keeps refrigerated for about a week.

Grilled Pumpkin

Ingredients
1 pumpkin (approx. 1kg), 5 tablespoons sesame oil, urine salt

Preparation
Cut the pumpkin in half and remove the seeds.

Place on the grill with the cut surfaces facing downwards and grill for 10-15 minutes.

Remove the pumpkin halves from the grill and brush the cut surfaces with sesame oil.

Now place the uncoated sides on the grill and grill again for about 30 minutes.

Spoon the pumpkin meat out of the skin and serve with a little oil and salt.

Tofu Fruit Skewers

Ingredients
300 g tofu, 4 skewers, 8 tbsp soy sauce, 2 tbsp water, 1 tsp ginger powder, 1/2 tsp curcuma, 1/2 tsp curry, red fruit or vegetables (red peppers, red onions, cherries, strawberries, etc.)

Preparation
Cut the tofu into cubes of two centimetres.

Mix the soy sauce, water and spices into a strong marinade and soak the tofu cubes in it for at least two hours. In addition to a good taste, they also assume a yellow colour.

Remove the tofu, drain well and fry all sides of the cubes until crispy. This can either be done with some oil in a pan (if the skewers are to be prepared) or on the grill.

Place the tofu cubes alternately with the red fruit or vegetable pieces on skewers and cook on the grill.

Grilled Steak

Ingredients
For the cooking broth
2 l water, 4 soy steaks, 3 tbsp vegetable stock powder, 2 tbsp paprika spice, sweet, some salt, freshly ground pepper

For the marinade
Salt, frying oil, paprika spice (hot), soy sauce, paprika spice, sweet, pepper, freshly ground, parsley (optional), spice mixture (optional). Soy flour (optional). Chili powder (optional), savory (optional)

Preparation
First the cooking broth
Bring 2 litres of water with vegetable stock powder and possibly other spices to the boil. The broth must be overgrown.

Let the soya steaks simmer for about 15 minutes until soft.

Then dry the steaks well with crepe paper.

Now the marinade (the fast variant)
Sprinkle the steaks with spices (e.g. salt, pepper, paprika, sweet and spicy, onion, garlic, savory and/or a mixture of spices) and rub in.

Sprinkle with soy sauce and rub in again. Now add enough frying oil and rub again.

Then turn the steaks over and season from the other side in the same way.

Then fry or grill the steaks.

The "I Have Time Variant"
In a bowl with a large surface, stir a marinade of fried oil, some soy sauce, soy flour and various spices (very

much: paprika sweet, much: paprika hot, pepper, salt, chili, onion, garlic, a little less: cumin, marjoram, oregano, parsley) or ready-made spice mixtures (gyros, steak, goulash, barbecue, chilli sin carne etc).

It is best to place the steaks in it completely covered with oil. The smaller the amount of oil, the more often it makes sense to stir the marinade and turn the steaks.

The longer the steaks are in there, the better they go through.

Let the steaks steep for 1-2 days, then they are optimal.

Steak again different

Ingredients
12 soy steaks, vegetable stock as required, 0.5 l beer, 400 ml vegetable oil, 2 onions, 4 tbsp mustard, 2 cloves garlic, rosemary, pepper, hot paprika powder, sweet paprika powder, nutmeg, sugar, chilli, optionally herbs of your choice

Preparation
Cook the soya steaks for 1/2 hour in a very strong vegetable broth. You can also make the broth almost twice as strong as indicated on the packaging.

Now peel the onions and garlic and cut both into small cubes.

Now for the marinade: Mix the remaining Ingredients in a bowl. Please do not use salt, as the vegetable broth is already sufficiently salted.

When the steaks are ready (they are soft and easy to cut) pour off the vegetable stock. Then put approx. 250 ml of the marinade into a freezer bag and put 3 still hot steaks into it.

Now leave to rest in the refrigerator for 24 hours or freeze as a supply.

Defrost before grilling (or take out of the fridge) and grill like normal steaks.

Marinade different:
In a bowl with a large surface, mix a marinade of fried oil, some soy sauce, soy flour and various spices (very much: paprika sweet, much: paprika hot, pepper, salt, chili, onion, garlic, rather less: cumin, marjoram, oregano, parsley).

Put the steaks completely covered with oil in it.

The smaller the amount of oil, the more often it makes sense to stir the marinade and turn the steaks. The longer the steaks are in there, the better they go through.

If you are in a hurry, you can fry or grill them after a few hours. If you have time, you can let them steep for 1-2 days, then they are optimal.

Now in the pan or on the grill.

Focaccia

Ingredients
250 g wheat flour, 1 teaspoon salt, 150 ml lukewarm water, 0.5 cubes yeast, 1 pinch sugar, 2 sprigs rosemary, salt flakes, olive oil

Preparation
Add the pinch of sugar to the lukewarm water, crumble the yeast into it and let it dissolve.

Pour the flour with the salt into a bowl, mix well, make a hollow in the middle and add the yeast water.

Now knead everything 5 minutes with your hands to a smooth dough and let it rise covered in a warm place for about 35 - 45 minutes.

Cover a baking tray with baking paper and divide the dough into four equal parts.

Now form four round focaccias and place them on the baking tray. Cover with a cloth and leave to rise for another 10 - 15 minutes. In the meantime, preheat the oven to 250 degrees.

Then press each focaccia several times into the top with your fingertips. Strip the rosemary needles from the branches, chop coarsely and sprinkle over the focaccia. Sprinkle the focaccia with salt flakes and drizzle with a little olive oil.

Now bake the focaccia on the bottom of the oven for about 13-15 minutes, then slide the baking tray onto the top rail of the oven and bake for 5 minutes until golden brown.

Fun Fact

Focaccia is a Ligurian flat bread made from yeast dough, which is topped with olive oil, salt and possibly herbs and other Ingredients before baking.

Potato Salad with Spring Onions

Ingredients
750 g waxy potatoes, 0.5 tbsp cumin, 180 ml vegetable stock, 5 tbsp white balsamic vinegar, 4 tbsp rapeseed oil, 1 tbsp medium hot mustard, 3 spring onions, salt, pepper

Preparation
Wash the potatoes, cover with water in a saucepan, add the caraway seeds and cook for 20-30 minutes, depending on the size.

Rinse the potatoes with cold water, peel and slice.

Mix the vegetable stock with half of the vinegar and season with salt and pepper, pour over the potatoes and mix carefully. Allow to stand for at least 30 minutes.

Prepare a dressing from the remaining vinegar, oil and mustard. Clean and wash the spring onions and cut them into fine rings.

Mix the dressing and spring onions with the salad. Season to taste and season if necessary.

Grilled Mushrooms

Ingredients
500 g fresh mushrooms, 4 cloves garlic, 5 tablespoons soy sauce, 5 tablespoons sunflower oil, some salt and pepper

Preparation
Clean the champions and put them aside first.

Press the garlic cloves through the garlic press or cut them into very small pieces and mix with the oil and soy sauce and season with salt and pepper.

Add the mushrooms and mix well. If there is not enough marinade, simply add some of the Ingredients.

Place in aluminium foil on the grill for a few minutes at a moderate heat, but do not close the foil at the top so that you can see whether the mushrooms are cooked.

Garlic Puree with Thyme

Ingredients
3 tubers garlic, 6 tablespoons olive oil, 6 stems fresh thyme, salt and pepper

Preparation
Sprinkle the garlic tubers (as they are - unpeeled) with 2 tablespoons of olive oil.

Add 2 stems of thyme and wrap in aluminium foil. Bake in the preheated oven on the middle shelf at 200 degrees (gas 3, convection oven 180 degrees) for 45-50 minutes.

Take out the garlic tubers and let cool a little. Then remove the toes from the tubers and press out the inside with your fingers.

Crush the garlic with a fork.

Stir in the remaining olive oil and season with salt and pepper. Pluck the leaves from the retained thyme, chop and mix into the garlic puree.

Cucumbers - Salsa

Ingredients
1 thick cucumber, 2 small diced onions, 5 tablespoons olive oil, for frying, 4 tablespoons apricot jam, 1 small lemon, the juice thereof, salt and pepper, from the mill, chilli, dried, from the mill

Preparation
Fry the onion cubes in olive oil until translucent.

Now add the apricot jam and the lemon juice. Season with salt, pepper and chilli and leave to cool.

In the meantime, peel the cucumber and cut into small cubes. Then stir in the onion mix and leave to stand in the fridge for about 1 hour.

Zucchini - Tomatoes - Onion - Skewers

Ingredients
4 onions, 8 cherry tomatoes, 2 courgettes, soy sauce, salt and pepper, freshly ground

Preparation
Peel the onions and cut into quarters.

Cut the courgettes into slices one centimetre thick.

Skewer zucchini, cherry tomatoes and onions alternately on wooden skewers. Season with salt and pepper and marinate with soy sauce.

Grill for 15 to 20 minutes, turning regularly.

Grilled Avocado

Ingredients
300 g tomatoes, 1 tsp Tabasco, 2 tablespoons Worcester sauce, 5 tablespoons olive oil, 4 stalks coriander green, 2 avocados, ½ lime, salt and pepper, sugar

Preparation
Cut the tomatoes into small cubes.

Mix Tabasco, Worcester sauce and 4 tablespoons olive oil, season with salt and 1 pinch of sugar. Coarsely chop coriander green and mix in.

Now add the tomato cubes to the sauce.

Halve the avocados lengthwise and remove the core.

Brush the avocado halves with lime juice and 1 tablespoon oil, salt and pepper.

Put the cut surface down on the not too hot grill (or grill pan) and grill for 4-5 minutes, turn and serve with the tomato cubes.

Grilled Courgette with Mint

Ingredients
3 courgettes, 1 handful fresh mint, first-class olive oil, coarse sea salt

Preparation
Wash the courgettes and cut off the end pieces.

Then cut lengthwise into thin slices.

Put some olive oil in a hot grill pan and put the zucchini slices into it and fry for about 5 minutes until they are slightly glassy and have a desirable grill pattern. That takes about five minutes from each side.

Now place the courgettes in an angular shape. When a layer is finished, sprinkle with coarse sea salt and place a few mint leaves on top.

Gradually grill the remaining courgette slices and layer them in the tin. At the end, place a few decorative mint leaves on top and spread a good dash of fine olive oil over them.

Allow to cool a little, then cover with foil and place in the refrigerator overnight.

Remove from the fridge about 1 hour before serving.

Baking

Chocolate - Nut - Coconut - Cake

Ingredients
250 g ground almond, 250 g ground grated coconut, or hazelnuts, 500 g flour, 500 g cane sugar, 2 sachets baking powder, 2 sachets vanilla sugar, 2 sachets cinnamon, 2 pinches salt, 6 tablespoons cocoa powder, 100 g margarine, 300 ml soy milk, 300 ml coffee or espresso, 2 grated carrots

Preparation
First mix all dry Ingredients well together.

Now slowly add the coffee and soymilk and mix thoroughly with the mixer. Please make sure that no lumps form.

Tip: If you add a finely grated carrot, the cake will be even juicier.

Place the mixture in a greased baking tin and preheat the oven to 180 degrees.

The baking time for top/bottom heat is approx. 60 minutes.

Of course, you can also add chopped dark chocolate (without milk), chopped nuts, cherries, etc.

Russian Plucked Cake

Ingredients
For the dough:
400 g flour, 200 g sugar, 240 g margarine, 2 sachets vanilla sugar, 2 sachets baking powder, 80 g dark cocoa, little soymilk or oat milk

For the cream:
400 g natural soy yoghurt, 2 pck. pudding powder (vanilla), 2 pck. vanilla sugar, 140 g sugar, some lemon juice

Preparation
First mix the Ingredients for the dough (but without the milk) with the mixer. If it is too dry, add some soymilk until it has the right consistency to line the springform pan.

Put a little dough aside for the crumbs and press the rest into the springform pan and form an edge. Place the springform pan in the refrigerator for one hour.

After approx. 50 minutes, preheat the oven to 160°C and mix the Ingredients for the cream.

Fill into the springform pan, form crumbs from the remaining dough and spread on the cream. Place in the oven for 40 - 45 minutes. Ready!

Vegan Walnut Cake

Ingredients
300 g flour, 250 ml soymilk, 200 g sugar, 150 ml oil, 1 pck baking powder, 1 pck vanilla sugar, 1 handful walnuts, 1 pck vegan cake icing (chocolate)

Preparation
Chop the walnuts, but not too fine. Place all Ingredients in a bowl and mix until smooth. Pour the dough into a cake tin.

Bake in a preheated oven at 200°C for approx. 25 minutes.

Melt the chocolate icing and spread it on the cake while it is still hot. Allow to cool.

Chocolate Mocha Cake

Ingredients
350 g silk tofu, not decanted, 2 tbsp safflower oil, 1 pinch salt, 450 g brown sugar, 5 tbsp high-quality cocoa powder, 5 tbsp soluble decaffeinated coffee, 1 tsp vanilla extract, 100 g wholemeal flour

Preparation
Beat the tofu with a hand mixer until creamy.

Mix with cocoa, oil, salt, sugar, coffee and vanilla. When the sugar has dissolved, fold in the flour.

Pour the dough into a 23 cm x 33 cm ovenproof dish.

Bake for 25-30 minutes until the cake separates from the baking tin.

Leave to cool in the baking tin and then cut into pieces with a clean, moist knife.

Red Wine Cake

Ingredients
200 g vegetable margarine, 250 g flour (e.g. wholemeal spelt mixed with wheat flour), 4 tablespoons soy flour, 8 tablespoons water, 200 g sugar, 1 sachet vanilla sugar, 1 sachet baking powder, 2 teaspoons cocoa powder (strongly de-oiled), 1 teaspoon cinnamon, 100 g dark chocolate without milk, 50 g chopped hazelnuts, 125 ml vegan red wine

Preparation
Mix all the Ingredients in a bowl with the mixer.

Cut the dark chocolate into very small pieces and fold in at the end.

Grease the cake tin well and bake the cake in the preheated oven at approx. 180°C hot air for about 40 minutes.

Orange Ccake

Ingredients
1 large orange, 200 g flour, 200 g sugar, 120 ml vegetable oil, 1 1/2 teaspoon baking soda, 1/4 teaspoon salt

Preparation
Preheat the oven to 190 C and grease a square (20 x 20 cm) baking tin.

Puree the orange pieces in a mixer and measure 240 ml of the orange juice and fruit flesh mixture.

Put the orange mixture, flour, sugar, oil, sodium bicarbonate and salt in a bowl and mix. Then pour the dough into the prepared mould.

Bake in a preheated oven for approx. 30 minutes.

Do the toothpick test: Put a toothpick into the dough. If no dough sticks to the toothpick, the cake is ready.

Chocolate Cake (gluten free)

Ingredients
For the dough:
3 tablespoons coconut, 220 g vegan gluten free biscuits, 2 tablespoons almond milk

For the topping:
4 g agar-agar, 60 ml boiling water, 120 g sugar, 30 g baked cocoa, 40 g corn starch, 70 ml almond milk, 60 g dark chocolate, minced, 1/2 tsp ground cardamom, finely grated peel of 1 orange

Preparation
Preheat the oven to 180°C.

Grease a flat round cake pan (also called pie pan) with vegetable oil.

Heat the coconut oil in a small pot to liquefy it.

Powder the biscuits in the food processor, add coconut oil and almond milk and make a crumbly mixture.

Distribute in the cake tin and press firmly, pressing up the dough at the edge.

Bake for 15 minutes in a preheated oven and then let cool.

In the meantime, place the agar-agar in a small bowl and pour 60 ml boiling water over it. Stir until it dissolves. Stand aside.

Put the baking cocoa, sugar and starch in a saucepan and heat over medium heat.

Stir in half of the almond milk with a whisk until the mixture is smooth. Then add the rest of the almond milk. Bring to the boil for about 10 minutes, stirring constantly, until the mixture thickens.

Remove the pot from the heat and fold in the chopped chocolate, cardamom, orange peel and agar-agar. Now stir until the chocolate has melted and the mixture is smooth.

Pour onto the pre-baked base and leave to set in the refrigerator for at least 3 hours.

Chocolate Cheesecake without baking

Ingredients
For the floor:
110 g walnuts, 40 g unsweetened cocoa powder, 200 g pitted dates, 1 tbsp vanilla extract, 1 pinch salt

For the stuffing:
360 g unsalted unsalted cashew nuts (soaked overnight in cold water, then poured off), 1.5 tsp vanilla extract, 165 g deep-frozen ripe bananas, 1 tbsp fresh lemon juice, 3 tbsp water, 1 pinch salt, 40 g unsweetened cocoa powder, 75 g pitted dates

Preparation
Start with the floor.

Chop the walnuts into coarse crumbs in a blender.

Add the remaining Ingredients for the base and mix until everything mixes well. Don't worry, the mixture will still be very crumbly after mixing.

Press about 200 g of the base mixture evenly into a 20 cm diameter cake springform pan lined with cling film. Stand aside.

Now for the filling: Put all the Ingredients for the filling in a bowl and puree until everything mixes well and the mixture is smooth.

Season to taste and if necessary, add more dates for more sweetness.

Then pour into a cake tin and smooth down with a damp spoon.

Cover with transparent film and place in the freezer for approx. 3 hours.

Once the cake has settled, it can be sliced and served.

Apple Pie with Cinnamon Sprinkles

Ingredients
205 g margarine, 350 g flour, 8 tbsp sugar, 1 packet vanilla sugar, 1 msp baking powder, 60 ml water, 2 tsp cinnamon, 750 g apples, 2 tbsp applesauce, fat, for the mould, flour, for the mould

Preparation
Please cut 125 g margarine into small pieces.

Mix 200 g flour, 2 tablespoons sugar, vanilla sugar and baking powder in a bowl.

Knead the margarine pieces, 60 ml water and the flour mixture until smooth. Wrap dough in foil and refrigerate for approx. 1 hour.

Knead 150 g flour, 6 tablespoons sugar, cinnamon and 80 g margarine into crumbles. Also, cool down.

Quarter apples, remove seeds, peel and cut into thin slices.

Pour the dough into a greased tart mould dusted with flour, preferably with a lift-off base, roll it out in the mould + press it up approx. 5 cm at the edge of the mould.

Then prick the bottom several times with a fork.

Spread the apples on the pastry base, heat the apple sauce and spread it on the apples.

Sprinkle with cinnamon crumble.

Bake in the preheated oven at 200°C top-bottom heat on the lower rack for approx. 40 minutes.

Marzipan Cake

Ingredients
For the dough:
175 g flour, 175 g margarine, 175 g sugar, 150 ml soymilk, alternatively oat or almond milk, 3 tbsp water, 40 g ground hazelnuts, 1 bag baking powder, 1 pinch salt, 1 pck vanilla pudding powder

For the cream:
1 sachet chilled and whipped soy cream, 250 ml oat or almond milk, 1 sachet vanilla pudding powder, 150 g marzipan, cut into pieces, 3 tbsp sugar

For the topping:
4 apples, 1 lemon, the juice thereof, 3 tbsp sugar, 1 sachet agar-agar

Besides:
1 pck. marzipan blanket, ready rolled out

Preparation
Mix all Ingredients for the dough with a mixer.

Cut the dough in half and bake in a medium-sized springform pan for 30 minutes at 180 degrees. Let it cool down afterwards.

Meanwhile for the pudding, stir the powder with a little soymilk and the sugar until smooth, bring the rest of the soymilk to the boil, stir in the mixed powder and the marzipan and bring to the boil.

If the marzipan doesn't dissolve completely, it's no big deal.

The pudding must now become cold and before it is added to the already whipped cream, it is briefly mixed once again with a blender jar so that no lumps form when the cream and pudding are mixed. Put the cream back in the fridge, please.

When the two sponge cake bases have cooled down, put the chopped apples together with the lemon juice and sugar in a pot and bring to the boil.

Shortly before boiling, add the agar-agar so that the whole thing becomes a jelly mass. Let simmer for three minutes and spread on one of the bases.

Once the apple mixture has cooled down, half of the marzipan cream can be spread on top.

Place the second layer on top and spread with cream again, not forgetting the edge.

After applying the paint, cool down a little before using the Marzipan blanket.

Carefully place the marzipan topping on the cake and press it down.

Cinnamon Stars

Ingredients
For the dough:
200 g icing sugar, 2 tbsp cinnamon powder, 8 tbsp water, 1 tbsp lemon juice, 150 g ground almonds, 200 g ground hazelnuts, 1 tbsp abrasion of orange peel

For the casting:
n. B. Powdered sugar, a little water, a little cinnamon powder

Preparation
Knead all the Ingredients for the dough firmly together.

Roll out on a surface covered with aluminum foil and cut out stars with a form.

Then let the stars dry at room temperature for about 4 hours.

After approx. 4 hours, bake the cinnamon stars on a baking tray lined with baking paper at 250°C for approx. 5 minutes. Do not leave too long in the oven, otherwise they will become too dry.

Let the cookies cool down well.

Make a thick icing from sifted icing sugar, cinnamon and a few drops of water.

Spread the icing on the cinnamon stars and let everything dry well. Ready!

Biscuit - Basic Recipe

Ingredients
225 g flour, 175 g sugar, 250 ml water, 4 tsp baking powder, 6 tbsp oil, 1 packet vanilla sugar, oil, for the dish

Optional
2 tbsp cocoa powder, if you want to make chocolate biscuits

Preparation
Put all the Ingredients for the dough in a large bowl. If you would like to make a chocolate biscuit, add the 2 tbsp cocoa powder.

Stir with a mixer until the dough is smooth and airy.

Grease a springform pan with some oil and preheat oven to 180°C.

Now pour the dough into the mould and put it into the oven for about 20 - 25 minutes.

You can do the test with a skewer or toothpick - stick it in and if no dough sticks, it's done. Let the cake cool.

Tip: It is well suited as a cake base or as a base for fruit cakes.

Chocolate Muffins

Ingredients
300 g flour, 50 g cocoa powder, 250 g sugar, 1 sachet baking powder, 7 tablespoons vegetable oil, 375 ml water, paper cups

Preparation
Preheat the oven to 170°.

Mix the flour well with cocoa powder, baking powder, sugar, oil and water.

Pour the dough into small muffin paper cups and bake for about 25-30 minutes.

Blueberry Muffins

Ingredients
150 g frozen blueberries, 1 big apple (if you don't like blueberries), 60 g cane sugar, 100 ml maize germ oil, rapeseed oil, or sunflower oil, 200 g spelt flour, 1/2 pck tartar baking powder, 1 pck vanilla sugar, 80 ml rice milk, 2 tablespoons maple syrup, paper cups

Preparation
Put sugar, flour, baking powder and vanilla sugar in a bowl and mix.

Then stir in the oil and rice milk.

Add 2 tablespoons maple syrup to the blueberries or the chopped apple (depending on which filling you prefer).

Pour half of the dough into the muffin moulds. Then add the fruit filling and the rest of the dough on top.

Bake the muffins at 160°C hot air for 25 minutes until they are slightly brown.

Cheesecake Muffins

Ingredients
For the dough: (chocolate dough)
170 g flour, 120 g cane sugar, 60 g cocoa powder, ½ Pck. vanilla sugar, 1 pck. baking powder, some baking soda, 220 ml soymilk, 50 ml rapeseed oil

For the dough: (Cheesecake mass)
250 g soy yoghurt, 45 g vegan margarine, 60 g cane sugar, ½ Pck. vanilla pudding powder, 6 tbsp soymilk, 3 tbsp soy flour, paper cups

Preparation
For the chocolate dough, put the flour, sugar, cocoa, vanilla sugar, baking powder and baking soda in a bowl and mix everything.

Now add the soymilk and the oil and work into a thick dough.

For the cheesecake mixture, mix the pudding powder, the soy flour and the soymilk. Please make sure that a viscous mass is formed. If it only makes a thick lump, add more milk.

Now add the remaining Ingredients and mix.

Preheat the oven to 180 degrees (circulating air).

Line the muffin tin with the paper muffins and always fill in 2 tbsp. chocolate dough. Then 2 tbsp. cheesecake mass and then 2 tbsp. chocolate dough again.

25 minutes in the oven.

Apple Muffins

Ingredients
1 cup sugar, 2 cups flour, 100 g ground almonds, 3 m. large grated apples, 1 m. large chopped apple, 1 cup oil, 1 cup sparkling apple spritzer, 1 pck baking powder, some cinnamon powder, paper moulds

Preparation
Mix all Ingredients except the chopped apple with a mixer. Finally add the chopped apple.

Pour the dough into a muffin tin lined with paper moulds.

Bake in a preheated oven at 160°C (top/bottom heat) for approx. 30 minutes.

Since the muffins are still very soft after baking and fall apart easily, let them cool down a little after baking.

Now remove from the mould.

Raisin Mares

Ingredients
250 ml soymilk, 50 g brown sugar, ½ yeast cube, 750 g flour, type 405, 20 g soy flour, 5 g salt, 1 Msp cinnamon powder, 80 g margarine, 110 ml water, 150 g raisins

Preparation
Dissolve the sugar and yeast in the soymilk and let it stand for 5 minutes.

Sieve the flour, soy flour, cinnamon and salt into a mixing bowl. Add the margarine, water and milk mixture and knead into a smooth dough for at least 5 minutes. Cover and let rest for 15 minutes.

Now knead the raisins under the dough and form a loaf from the dough.

Press the externally visible raisins into the loaf with one finger. The resulting holes close again automatically as they open.

Place the loaf on a baking tray lined with baking paper and cover with a tea towel. Spray the towel with water and allow the dough to rise at room temperature for approx. 60-90 minutes until it has significantly enlarged.

Preheat the oven to 200° top/bottom heat and bake the mares in the lower third of the oven for 30 minutes until golden brown.

Allow to cool on a grid.

Pita - Bread with Sesame Seeds

Ingredients
300 ml lauwarmes water, 1 pck. dry yeast, 1 teaspoon salt, 450 g flour, sesame seeds for sprinkling, some water for spreading

Preparation
Mix water, yeast, salt and flour, knead well and leave to rise for about 45 minutes.

Now form 10 round, flat, approx. 0.5 cm thick pieces from the dough and place them on a baking tray lined with baking paper.

Leave to rise for 5 minutes and then brush the "rolls" with a little water and sprinkle with the sesame seeds.

Bake in a preheated oven at 225°C for approx. 10 minutes.

Serve immediately or freeze for storage.

Fun Fact
Pita, Pide in Turkey, is a slightly thicker, soft pita bread made from yeast dough and spread from Greece to the Middle East. It serves, freshly baked several times a day, as a side dish with almost all meals.

Pizza Bread

Ingredients
For the dough
500 g flour, type 550, 250 ml water, 4 g fresh yeast, 2 tablespoons olive oil, ½ tablespoon salt, ½ TL sugar

For the covering
6 tbsp. olive oil, 6 tsp. mixed Mediterranean herbs (e.g. rosemary, basil, oregano), 1 tsp. sea salt

Preparation
Knead all the Ingredients for the dough well (by hand or with a mixer).

Allow to rise for 1 hour at room temperature.

Remove about 120 g dough per pizza bread, spread a little, let rest for 10 minutes.

Roll out on a floured base. Leave to rest for another 10 minutes and roll out again. To prevent the dough from blistering, prick it with a fork.

Cover the dough with olive oil, sprinkle over the herbs and salt lightly.

Now preheat oven to 220° C

Bake the pizza bread in the oven for 10 minutes. But please make sure that the bread does not get too dark.

The rest of the dough can be stored in the refrigerator for up to 7 days.

Tip: The quantities are variable. Garlic olive oil can also be used for dressing.

Baguette Parisienne

Ingredients
400 g flour, type 405, 1 ½ TL salt, ¼ TL dry yeast, 320 ml water

Preparation
Mix flour, salt and yeast in a bowl.

Add water and mix in just enough so that there are no more dry nests. However, please do not use a machine for stirring, but do everything nicely by hand.

Cover the bowl with foil and leave to cool for 12-16 hours. After this time a dough mass with many bubbles has formed.

Now dust a worktop well with flour and slide the dough onto the floured worktop using a dough scraper. Do not knead the dough, but divide it into three equal parts. Make three baguettes out of them and place them in a baguette baking tin.

These baking tins are approx. 37 cm long and suitable for 3 baguettes.

Leave to rise in the baguette baking tin until the dough has filled the tin well.

Bake in the preheated oven at 250°C top/bottom heat for 10 -15 minutes on the middle shelf.

Tip: After you have placed the baguettes in the oven, spray the bottom of the oven with a flower spray of water. This produces a particularly beautiful crust of bread.

Gingerbread

Ingredients
3 T wholemeal flour, 1 ½ TL baking soda, 1 pck. ground almonds, 1 ¼ T sugar, 1 pck. Vanilla sugar, 2 tsp cinnamon, 1 Msp clove powder, 1 Msp mace, ½ TL cardamom, ½ TL pimento, 1 lemon (the grated peel thereof), 1 ½ T soy milk, 5 tbsp unsweetened apple sauce, 2 tbsp oil, 3 tbsp sugar beet syrup, 3 tbsp starch, 3 tbsp soy flour, 50 wafers (diameter 7.5 cm)

Preparation
Place the flour, baking soda, sugar, vanilla sugar, spices and the grated lemon zest in a bowl and mix well.

Add the soymilk, applesauce, oil and sugar beet syrup and knead together.

Add the starch and soy flour last and knead well until the dough is even.

Now preheat the oven to 180°C.

Add approx. one tablespoon of dough to each wafer. Make sure that you leave a margin, as the dough still expands during baking).

Place the wafers with the gingerbread dough on a baking tray lined with baking paper and bake at 180°C for approx. 20 minutes.

When the baking time is over, place the gingerbread on a cake rack and let it cool down.

Tip: Instead of ground almonds you can also use ground hazelnuts.

Fruit Bbread

Ingredients
7-8 apples, 150g raisins, 150g dried figs, 250g sugar, ½ Pck. Gingerbread spice, 1 pee. tablespoon cocoa, 1 teaspoon cinnamon, 100g whole hazelnuts, 2 teaspoons baking soda, 500g flour, some margarine to grease the baking tin

Preparation
Peel the apples, remove the core and then grate them into a bowl.

Cut the figs into small cubes and add to the grated apple.

Add raisins, sugar, gingerbread spice, cinnamon and cocoa, mix well.

Leave the dough to stand overnight in the covered bowl in the refrigerator.

The next morning (or late afternoon if you need to work) add flour and baking soda, knead well with your hands.

Now knead all the hazelnuts with the dough.

Grease a large baking pan and add the dough.

Bake at 180°C for approx. 80 minutes.

Tip: Instead of dried figs, dried apricots or other dried fruits may also be used.

Covered Apple Pie

Ingredients
For the dough:
250g soft margarine, 200g sugar, 6 tablespoons ground hazelnuts, 1 teaspoon baking soda, 220g light wheat flour, 100g whole wheat flour, ½ teaspoon cinnamon, 1 pinch salt

For the stuffing:
10 sour apples, 1 tbsp lemon juice, 4 tbsp ground hazelnuts, 100g raisins, 1 tsp cinnamon, 2 tbsp sugar, 3 tbsp chopped almonds

Preparation
Knead the margarine, sugar, hazelnuts, baking soda, flour, cinnamon and salt in a bowl into a dough.

Then form the dough into a ball and let it rest covered in the refrigerator for at least 1/2 hour.

Peel and eighth the apples, remove the core and cut the apple pieces into 1/2 cm thick slices and sprinkle with lemon juice. Add hazelnuts, raisins, cinnamon, sugar, almonds and mix everything.

Line the bottom and edge of a well greased springform pan (28cm) with rolled out shortcrust pastry and place the apple mixture on top.

Place the rest of the rolled out shortcrust pastry on top of the apple mixture as a "lid".

Preheat the oven to 175°C. Bake at 175°C on the middle rack for approx. 70-80 minutes.

Oat Biscuits

Ingredients
100g soft margarine, 1 ½ T tender oat flakes, 1 ½ T wholemeal flour, 1 teaspoon baking soda, 4 tablespoons sugar beet syrup, ½ T soymilk, 100g raisins, 100g chopped almonds or hazelnuts, 1 small banana, fat for the form

Preparation
Mix the margarine well with the oat flakes, then add the flour and baking soda and mix.

Wrap the sugar beet syrup around the spoon and add to the oatmeal mixture.

Now add soymilk, raisins and nuts or almonds and knead well.

Puree the banana and knead with the rest of the dough.

To allow the oat flakes to swell, leave the dough covered for approx. 20 minutes.

Grease a baking tray and form the dough with a tablespoon into small piles, which you then place on the baking tray.

Preheat the oven to 175°C.

Bake at 175°C for approx. 20 minutes.

Remove the oat biscuits from the tray and leave to cool on a cake rack.

Raspberry Pudding Cake

Ingredients
For the floor:
250 g flour, ½ Pck. dry yeast, 50 g sugar, 1 tablespoon margarine, 100 ml soymilk

For the topping:
2 ½ T soymilk, 1 tablespoon oil, 1 sachet vanilla sugar, ½ T sugar, 2 teaspoons agar, 3 ass. EL starch, 300 g fresh or frozen raspberries, cake ring recommended

Preparation
First mix the bottom: flour and yeast in a bowl.

Heat margarine, sugar and soymilk in a saucepan until the sugar has dissolved and the margarine has melted. Please make sure it doesn't get too hot. Now add this to the flour in the bowl process it to a dough.

Let it go for 30 minutes.

Grease a round baking tin (25cm diameter) with margarine and cover the base with dough.

Preheat the oven to 180°C.

Now bake the dough for 20 minutes and let it cool down.

Now for the topping: Mix the agar with some cold water in a pot, then boil with 2 cups soymilk, vanilla sugar, sugar, 1 tablespoon oil for 2 minutes.

Dissolve the starch in ½ T soymilk and add to the pot.

Cook for 2 minutes, stirring again and again. Allow to cool for approx. 15 minutes.

Now add the raspberries, stir briefly.

Spread the mixture on the cake base (use cake ring). Cool and allow to set in the refrigerator.

Potato Bbread

Ingredients
3 floury potatoes, 500g light wheat flour (type 520 or 1050), 2 tbsp starch, 1/2 pkg dry yeast, 2 teaspoons sugar, 1/3 t lukewarm water, 1/2 t lukewarm soymilk, 2 teaspoons salt

Preparation
Cook the potatoes, peel them, crush the potatoes with the potato mashers and let them cool.

Dissolve yeast and sugar in water, leave to rise for 15 minutes.

Knead everything with the remaining Ingredients (also with the potatoes) for about 10 minutes.

Leave to rise covered for three quarters of an hour.

Form a loaf and place it on baking paper.

Leave in the oven at the lowest temperature for another 10-15 minutes.

Now turn up the oven to 200°C and bake for about 45-50 minutes.

Carrot Cake

Ingredients
5 carrots, 1 ½ T sugar, 3 T flour, 1 lemon, 250g margarine, 1 Msp cinnamon, 1 teaspoon baking soda, 8-10 tablespoons icing sugar, oil

Preparation
Peel and grate the carrots. Grate the lemon zest into it.

Add the sugar, flour, margarine, cinnamon and baking soda and knead.

Now put everything into a greased box form.

Preheat oven to 180°C.

Bake at 180°C for 45 minutes.

Allow to cool a little and turn out of the mould.

Squeeze out the lemon and stir the juice with icing sugar until smooth.

Spread the glaze on the still warm cake.

Cherry Crumble

Ingredients
For the floor:
3 t flour, 3/4 t sugar, 150g margarine, 2 go. tbsp. soy flour, 6 tbsp. water, 1 pr. salt, 1 sachet baking powder, 1 1/2 tb soy or oat milk, 1 sachet vanilla sugar

For the cherry filling:
700 ml sour cherries, 2 pck. vanilla sugar, 2 pck. vanilla pudding powder, if required sugar

For the sprinkles:
125 g margarine, 2 T flour, 1 T sugar, 100g ground almonds, 1 pr cinnamon, fat for the baking tray

Preparation
Let's start with the bottom: Put the sugar and margarine in a bowl and beat until foamy.

Then add flour, salt, baking powder, soymilk and vanilla sugar and mix everything together.

Mix the soy flour well with the water, add to the dough and mix.

Grease a baking tray and spread the dough on it.

Now for the cherry filling: For the cherry filling, put the sour cherries in a saucepan except for a little juice. Add vanilla sugar and bring to the boil.

Mix the pudding powder with the remaining cherry juice and add to the boiling cherry mixture. Bring to the boil briefly, then remove from the heat and allow to cool slightly.

Now the sprinkles: Knead all the Ingredients for the sprinkles together.

Spread the cherry mixture on the base and crumble the sprinkles on top.

Bake at 175°C for approx. 40 minutes.

The cake is ready when the edges are golden brown.

Coconut Cookies

Ingredients
100 g coconut flakes, 125 g margarine, 100 g sugar, 200 g wheat flour, 4 tbsp coconut milk, 1 pinch salt, grated coconut (optional)

Preparation
Mix all the Ingredients together and knead into a smooth dough (if the dough is too dry, add a little more liquid).

Cover and keep cold for half an hour.

Now roll out the mixture thinly on a baking paper and cut out in rhombuses.

Decorate with grated coconut if desired.

Bake at 190°C for 15-20 minutes.

Pumpkin Seed Bread

Ingredients
500g wholemeal wheat flour, 2 T lukewarm water, 2 T oat flakes, 1 cube yeast, 4 tbsp pumpkin seeds, 1 tbsp raw sugar, 2-3 tbsp soymilk, 1 tbsp lemon juice or vinegar, 1 tbsp salt, oil to grease the baking tin

Preparation
Dissolve yeast and sugar in 1/2 t water and leave in a warm place for 20 minutes.

After approx. 20 minutes mix with the remaining Ingredients and stir well. Grease a box mould and add the dough.

Leave in the oven at 50°C for 45 minutes.

Bake at 220°C for 30 minutes, then at 190°C for 45 minutes.

Spray with water every 20-30 minutes.

Tip: Replace pumpkin seeds with linseed, sunflower seeds, nuts, etc. Use spelt flour as a substitute for wheat flour.

Covered Plum Cake

Ingredients
For the dough:
500 g spelt flour, ¼ l cold water, ½ yeast cubes, 3-4 tbsp agave syrup, 1 pinch of whole sea salt, 2 tbsp sunflower oil or safflower oil

For the topping:
2 kg plums, 600 g coarsely ground almonds, 4-5 tablespoons agave syrup, 3 Msp. natural vanilla, juice and peel of 1/2 - 1 lemon

Preparation
Let's start with the dough: dissolve yeast in water, add agave syrup, sea salt and oil, mix well.

Add the spelt flour and knead well for about 8 minutes.

Roll out the dough on a floured tray.

Now let's get to the topping: remove the seeds from the plums, cut them in half and cut them 2 x into the top, then spread them over the dough.

Mix the remaining Ingredients well and spread over the plums. Press on well with your hands.

In the oven, on the 2nd rail from below, bake for a total of 35 minutes at 160°C circulating air, 20 minutes of which uncovered and 15 minutes covered with baking paper. You can weigh down the upper baking paper with saucers.

Onion Tart

Ingredients
For the dough:
150 g wheat, finely ground, 100 g rye, finely ground, ½ TL coriander, ground, 20 g yeast, 1 TL cane sugar, approx. 1/8 l water, ½ TL salt, 4 tbsp olive oil, some oil for the baking tray

For the topping:
500 g onions, 150 g mushrooms, 1 bunch parsley, 250 g tofu, herb salt, pepper, oil for braising

Preparation
First the dough: Put the flour in a bowl and press a hollow in the middle.

Dissolve the yeast with the sugar in a little warm water, add to the trough and mix to a pre-dough.

Cover and leave to rise in a warm place for 15 minutes.

Add the remaining Ingredients and so much warm water that the dough separates from the bowl.

Keep beating the dough until it blows bubbles.

Cover with a kitchen towel and allow to rise until the dough has doubled. Then roll out on an oiled baking tray and allow to rise again.

While the dough is going, peel the onions and cut them into rings, clean the mushrooms and cut them into slices and steam both in oil until the onions are glassy.

Chop the parsley and puree together with the tofu. Add enough water to make the mixture easy to spread.

Season to taste with herb salt and pepper.

Now mix the tofu mixture with the onions and mushrooms and spread over the dough.

Finally bake at 220°C for 30 minutes on medium shelf.

Oat Flake Nut Biscuits

Ingredients
150 g finely ground oat, 150 g oat flakes, 150 g margarine, 150 g chopped cashew nuts, 100 g cane sugar, 100 g carob, 1sp baking soda, 1sp salt, 1 tsp carob bean gum, a little soymilk

Preparation
Mix and knead oat flour, oat flakes, baking soda, carob bean gum, carob, salt and margarine together.

Knead the chopped cashew nuts and cane sugar into the dough.

Add so much soymilk that the mixture does not become crumbly.

Form small piles of dough with two teaspoons and place on a greased baking tray.

Then bake at 175°C for approx. 15-20 minutes.

Tortillas

Ingredients
250g flour (type 405), 250ml boiling water, ½ TL salt, 50g flour to roll out

Preparation
Put the flour with the salt in a bowl and form a hollow in the middle. Pour the boiling water into the well and stir with a wooden spoon. After a few seconds, continue kneading the hot dough with your hands.

Without further waiting time directly after kneading, divide into six portions and roll each into a flat cake. Fry in a coated pan from each side for about one minute. Please do this without adding fat.

Tip: Results in six tortillas and goes well with paprika humus and cheese, among other things.

Banana Bread

Ingredients
80 g margarine, 150 g sugar, 400 g flour, 2 teaspoons baking powder, 3 ripe crushed bananas, 120 ml soy drink, 1 teaspoon vanilla extract, 40 g walnuts, chopped

Preparation
Preheat the oven to 150 degrees.

Now melt the margarine with the sugar in a pot. Then first stir the flour and baking powder into the pot, then gradually add all other Ingredients and mix well.

Now grease the box mould (11x28 cm) and fill in the dough.

Bake the bread in the preheated oven for about 50 minutes.

Coarse Rye Bread

Ingredients
400 g rye flour (type 997), 400 ml water, 80 g sourdough

For the dough:
400 g rye flour (type 997), 300 g wheat flour (type 550), 3 tsp. salt, 800 g sourdough (prepared mixture), 2 g yeast, depending on sourdough activity, 300 ml lukewarm water, flour for the fermentation baskets

Preparation
For the sourdough mixture, stir 400 g rye flour, 400 ml water and the sourdough together and leave at room temperature overnight (approx. 18 - 20 hours).

Mix the two types of flour (400 g rye flour and 300 g wheat flour) and press a hollow into the middle. Put the salt on the edge and the yeast in the trough.

Add lukewarm water and the sourdough mixture to the trough.

Now knead everything together with the dough hook for approx. 10 minutes.

Let the dough rest for 30 minutes.

Put the dough on the work surface and knead vigorously, divide into 2 portions and put them into floured fermenting baskets.

After 60 minutes, place the bread on a baking tray and bake in the oven preheated to 250°C.

In the first 15 minutes, sharpen about 3 times with a finely adjusted flower tip on the walls of the oven, but not on the bread.

After 15 minutes, reduce the heat of the oven to 200°C and bake the bread for approx. 60 minutes.

10 minutes before the end of the baking time, open the oven a little (clamp the kitchen towel or wooden spoon between door and oven) and finish baking.

The bread should sound hollow at the bottom, if you knock against it, then it is ready.

Tip: If you like, you can add feta cheese and/or pepperoni to a dough portion. Of course, before baking. This recipe is enough for 2 small rye breads of 750 g each.

Wholemeal Bread

Ingredients
500 g wholemeal flour

100 g seeds (sesame, linseed, sunflower seeds), 500 ml water, 1 teaspoon salt, 1 teaspoon sugar, 1 1/2 pck. dry yeast, fat for the form

Preparation
Place all **Ingredients** in a bowl and stir well with a dough hook (5 - 10 minutes).

Pour the dough into a greased box mould (30cm diameter).

Leave to rise for about 1 hour until the volume of the dough has doubled.

Cut in between to avoid cavities.

Preheat the oven to 250°C 15 minutes before the end of the walking time. Place the box mould in the preheated oven (centre) on a grid.

Now bake the bread for 25 minutes.

If the bread becomes too dark, please reduce the heat to 200 - 220°C.

When the baking time is up, take the bread out of the tin and place it on a grill.

Allow to cool for 2 hours.

Buns

Ingredients
300 g flour (wheat flour type 550), 50 g durum wheat semolina, 150 g wholemeal spelt flour, 1 tsp salt, 1/2 pck dry yeast, 325 g lukewarm water, fat for the baking tray

Preparation
Knead all the Ingredients to a smooth dough.

Now form the dough into a ball and place in a warm place for 45 minutes and let rest.

After the 45-minute rest, take the dough out of the bowl and divide it into 8 equal parts.

These 8 parts are now formed into rolls.

Place the rolls on a greased baking tray and cut them lengthwise with a sharp knife and cover with a kitchen towel.

Now preheat the oven to 250°C.

If the oven is hot, spray the rolls with water with a flower spray until they shine moist.

Place in the oven and bake for about 20 minutes until golden brown.

Pumpkin - Olives - Rosemary - Bread

Ingredients
350 g Hokkaido pumpkin, coarsely grated, 600 g wholemeal flour, 100 g spelt flour, 3 tsp salt, 1 cube yeast, 200 ml water, 1 tbsp olive oil, 2 tbsp fresh finely chopped rosemary, 5 tbsp pumpkin seeds, roasted without fat and coarsely chopped, 100 g black olives, coarsely chopped, fat for the form

Preparation
Stir the yeast with a little water until smooth and then let it stand for 10 minutes.

Mix flour, salt and pumpkin.

Add the yeast mixture, olive oil and water, stir in (the amount of water depends on the humidity of the pumpkin meat) and knead into a smooth dough.

Cover and leave to rise for approx. 1 hour.

Add rosemary, pumpkin seeds and olives (all small cracked) and knead in.

Put the dough in a greased box mould and let it rise for 30 minutes.

Preheat the oven to 220°C and bake the bread for about 40 minutes.

Tip: After 1-2 days it tastes even better than freshly baked, because the bread gets wet through the pumpkin and the aromas of the spices come into their own.

Wholemeal roll with Carrots and Sunflower Seeds

Ingredients
400 g wheat flour (whole grain) or whole grain spelt flour, 100 g wheat flour or spelt flour, type 405 or 550, 25 g wheat gluten, 20 g fresh yeast, 330 ml lukewarm water, 10 g sea salt, 1 tsp sugar beet syrup, 15 g butter, 300 g carrot, coarsely grated, 100 g lightly roasted sunflower seeds

Preparation
Mix the two kinds of flour and the glue in a bowl, press a hollow in the middle and pour in the water.

Crumble the yeast into the trough and mix with the sugar beet syrup to a soft pre-dough. The best way to do this is to use a fork. Always stir some flour from the edge into the dough until you think the consistency is right.

Now cover the bowl and leave to rise for 25 minutes.

In the meantime, melt the butter in a large pan and steam the grated carrots for about 5 minutes so that the carrots lose some of their liquid.

Add the grated carrots, sunflower seeds and salt to the pre-dough and knead everything for 10 minutes by hand or with a food processor.

Cover the bowl with a foil and a cloth and let the dough rise for another 30 - 40 minutes.

After the resting period, turn the dough onto a floured surface and knead again briefly.

Cut off rolls weighing approx. 70g and let them rest for a moment.

Now push the flour aside on the floured surface. At this point, turn the rolls in your hollow hand into round rolls.

Place on a baking tray at a distance of 3-4 cm. Cover with a floured foil and leave to rise for another 20-25 minutes.

Now heat up the stove.

Moisten well with a flower syringe and bake at 230°C.

Pour a cup of hot water onto the bottom of the oven and close the door immediately.

After 5 minutes, reduce to 200-210 degrees and bake for another 20 minutes.

Cereal Rolls

Ingredients
400 ml warm water, 1 cube yeast, 1 pinch salt, 250 g whole wheat, 200 g spelt flour, 100 g flour (type 405), 140 g plums, dried, 115 g apricots, dried, 70 g dates, dried, 40 g hazelnuts, partly chopped, ground or whole, 30 g sesame seeds, 40 g linseed, 50 g sunflower seeds, 100 g oat flakes, 2 tsp salt, 2 tbsp vinegar, 2 tbsp oat flakes for sprinkling, 2 tbsp sunflower seeds or mixed seeds

Preparation
Dissolve the yeast cube in 300 ml of warm water and add the pinch of sugar.

Mix the flours with the salt.

Add the oat flakes, sesame seeds, linseed, sunflower seeds and nuts to the flour.

Cut the dried fruit into small pieces and mix in as well.

Add the vinegar and the sugared yeast water and mix well with the dough hooks. Slowly add the remaining 100 ml of water so that the dough absorbs all the **Ingredients** well but does not stick.

Now knead well again with your hands, then cover and leave to rise in a warm place for approx. 1 hour.

When the dough has enlarged, knead again with your hands and form 12 rolls.

Place the rolls on a baking tray lined with baking paper, sprinkle with oat flakes and seeds and press them down well.

Cover the tray with a towel and let the rolls rise for another 1/2 to 3/4 hour.

Preheat the oven to 180°C during this time.

Bake the rolls on the middle shelf for a total of 25 minutes at top and bottom heat.

After 15 minutes switch from top/bottom heat to circulating air.

Tip: Those who prefer a crispy crust should place a cup of boiling water on the bottom of the oven during the baking process.

Tomato and Olive Ciabatta

Ingredients
800g wheat flour, 200g Wholemeal flour, 300g lukewarm water, 2 teaspoons salt, 1 glass of olives marinated in herb oil, ½ glass of dried tomatoes marinated in oil, 4 tablespoons olive oil, 3. pck dry yeast, a little more for the worktop, some olive and tomato oil to brush on

Preparation
First, mix the flour with the lukewarm water, the salt and the yeast to form a light dough.

Now mix in the olive oil. To make the dough even smoother, knead it with your hands for a short time. If the dough is still too moist, add a little more flour. If it is too dry, increase the amount of water slightly. That always depends on what kind of flour they use.

Now divide the dough into two parts. Put the olives in the first one and knead them into the dough.

Add the dried tomatoes cut into small pieces to the other. Knead well into the dough again. Put the oil in which the tomatoes were stored aside, because you'll need it right away.

Now put the two dough balls in a bowl and cover them with a kitchen towel and let them rest for about 45 minutes.

After the resting period, please preheat the oven to 200°C.

Now form two loaves from the two dough balls and spread the dough with the olives, with olive oil and the dough with the tomatoes, with the oil from the glass in which the tomatoes were marinated.

When the oven has reached the desired temperature, the breads are placed in the oven for about 30 - 40 minutes.

The breads are ready when they have a light brown crust.

Disclaimer

The implementation of all information, instructions and strategies contained in this e-book is at your own risk. The author cannot assume any liability for any damages of any kind for any legal reason. Liability claims against the author for material or immaterial damage caused by the use or non-use of information or by the use of incorrect and/or incomplete information are fundamentally excluded. Any legal claims and claims for damages are therefore excluded. This work has been compiled and written down with the greatest care to the best of our knowledge and belief. For the topicality, completeness and quality of the information the author does not take over however any guarantee. Also misprints and false information cannot be excluded completely. No legal responsibility or liability in any form can be assumed for incorrect information provided by the author.

Copyright

All contents of this work as well as information, strategies and tips are protected by copyright. All rights reserved. Any reprint or any reproduction - even in extracts - in any form like photocopy or similar processes, storage, processing, duplication and distribution by means of electronic systems of any kind (in whole or in extracts) is strictly prohibited without the express written permission of the author. All translation rights reserved. Under no circumstances may the contents be published. In case of disregard, the author reserves the right to take legal action.

Imprint

© Jonathan M. Hiemer

2019

1st edition

All rights reserved

Reprinting, even in extracts, not permitted

No part of this work may be reproduced, duplicated or distributed in any form or by any means without the written permission of the author.

Contact: hiemerjonathan@gmail.com

Cover design: lauria @ fiverr

Printed in Germany
by Amazon Distribution
GmbH, Leipzig